Minimalism

Live a Meaningful Life

JOSHUA FIELDS MILLBURN
& RYAN NICODEMUS

...tana

Published by Asymmetrical Press.

The best way to organize your stuff is to get rid of most of it.

Library of Congress Cataloging-in-Publication Data
Minimalism: live a meaningful life / Millburn, Nicodemus — 2nd ed.
Print ISBN: 978-0615648224
eISBN: 978-1936539673
WC: 30,635
1. Minimalism. 2. Happiness. 3. The Minimalists.
4. Simplicity. 5. Consumerism. 6. Self-help. 7. Careers.

Photography by Joshua Weaver
Cover design by Dave LaTulippe, SPYR
Typeset in Garamond by Shawn Mihalik
Edited by Shawn Harding
Formatted in beautiful Montana
Printed in the U.S.A.

Disclaimer: persons considering changing their diet or exercise regimens should consult a physician before implementing any diet or exercise program.

ASYM METR ICAL

For Chloe & Eric

It is not things that disturb us,
but our interpretation of their significance.

—EPICTETUS

CONTENTS

minimalism: live a meaningful life

Are you truly happy?

FOREWORD

A Brief Introduction

Conformity is the drug with which many people self-medicate. Not happy? Buy this. Buy that. Buy something. Keep up with the Joneses, the Trumps, the Kardashians. After all, you can be just like them, right?

Clearly this is wrong. We all know this, and yet we continue to try. Day in, day out, we try. We try to keep up, try to measure up, try to live up to societal expectations. We place immense pressure on ourselves to be something—or someone—we are not.

Consequently, people are more stressed than ever. We have more pressure put on us than any other time in history. You see it on TV: the toothpick-thin models and rugged "sexiest men alive" dominating the screen. *This* is what you're *supposed* to look like. You hear it on the radio, the solipsistic, overindulgent Hummer-driving rap stars and champagne-guzzling pop stars promulgating irresponsible living. *This* is how you're *supposed* to consume. You notice it at work, the coworker gossip about him and her and, god forbid, *you*. *This* is how you're *supposed* to behave. To have the tallest building in town, you must tear down everyone else's.

Suffice it to say, the pressure surrounds us.

Or does it?

The truth is that nearly all the pressure we feel is completely internal. Sure, this pressure is influenced by external factors, but that doesn't mean we have to take the bait. We needn't succumb to these influences. Because even if you could be a Kardashian or a Trump or a Jones, it wouldn't make you happy. Happiness comes from within, from inside yourself, from living a meaningful life. And that is what this book aims to help you discover.

About The Minimalists

This book is ultimately about *you* and how *you* can live a meaningful life. But let's talk about us for a moment.

We are Joshua Fields Millburn & Ryan Nicodemus—a pair of thirty-somethings who write essays about living a meaningful life with less stuff at *TheMinimalists.com*, a website with more than 4 million readers. Our story has been featured on the *Today* show, *Wall Street Journal*, *New York Times*, *USA Today*, *Forbes*, *Time* magazine, *People* magazine, and many other outlets. We both have extensive experience leading large groups of people in corporate America, coaching and developing hundreds of employees to help them grow as individuals and contribute to the world around them.

Once upon a time, we were two happy young professionals living in Dayton, Ohio. But we weren't *truly* happy. We were best friends in our late twenties, and we both had great six-figure jobs, fancy cars, big houses, expensive clothes, plenty of toys—an abundance of stuff. And yet with all this stuff, we knew we weren't satisfied with our lives; we weren't fulfilled. We discovered that working 70 or 80 hours a week, and buying even more stuff, didn't fill the void—it widened it. So we took back control of our lives using the principles of minimalism to focus on what's important.

About This Book

This book has been a long time in the making. Its initial iteration, conceived in 2010 and completed in March 2011, resulted in a 300-page how-to guide called *Minimalism in 21 Days*. A *300-page* book about becoming a minimalist? This didn't feel right to us. How could a book about minimalism—a book about reducing life's excess—be 300 pages? We could almost taste the irony. Don't get us wrong, it was a *good* book, far better than most drivel you'll find on the Internet. But because we didn't feel it was a *great* book, and because it lacked a necessary brevity, we did what any responsible authors would've done: we scrapped the entire project, published an attenuated version of *Minimalism in 21 Days* on our website (minimalists.com/21days), and started over with a blank page. It was difficult, but it felt like the only genuine way to create a meaningful book.

The result was the first edition of *Minimalism: Live a Meaningful Life*, published in 2011 by Asymmetrical Press. Much has happened, and many lessons have been learned, in the five years since we published that first edition. Hence, the book you are reading now: the second edition of *Minimalism*.

While re-reading this short book to write this updated edition, we were astonished by how well the book's principles have endured. During every event, every interview, and nearly every conversation we have with readers, we find ourselves returning to the Five Values in this book. While we won't use the pages of this new edition to expand on the past half-decade (our memoir, *Everything That Remains*, and our essay collection, *Essential*, do a thorough job of that), we significantly updated *Minimalism* by expanding on the Five Values expressed in this book.

Our website provides the ultimate how-to-start guide for free, as well as frequent updates by way of our online essays, which explore minimalism at a deep level, detailing practical ways to apply simple living to your life. We wrote this book to be used in a similar, practical way (we certainly don't want to waste your time). The ingredients in this book are designed to provide you with a basic recipe for intentional living, while allowing you to adjust the recipe to suit your own taste and lifestyle. Furthermore, while this entire book can be consumed within a day or two, it is organized into seven succinct chunks, which are better digested in a week, one chapter at a time.

This book is different from the content on our website and in our other books. While our website documents our journey into minimalism and our continued growth through experimentation, this book discusses minimalism in a different way: it covers in depth the Five Values for living a meaningful life. It also provides insight into our personal lives, including the painful events that led us to our journey into minimalism.

The book itself is written and organized to help you think about your life and how you live it; to make you do some work and introspection so you can step away from your old life and journey into a new one; to help you realize you can change, you can re-select who you're going to be, you can become the best person you're capable of becoming—the real you, the passionate, loving, compassionate, disciplined, happy *you*. So, if you truly want to maximize what you learn from this book, we ask you not only read its content, but also do three things as you read:

Read more than once. The first reading primes the pump, but re-reading the parts you find most relevant will fuel your desire to take action to change your life.

Take notes. Unlike the essays on our website, this book is not designed to be read just once. And it is not a theoretical document. We want you to get the most out of this book, which means taking notes, highlighting certain passages, and making lists to help you better understand yourself.

Take action. This is the most important step. If you read this book but do nothing with what you've learned, then you are wasting your time. It's fine to just absorb the information to start, but *action* is what's going to change your life. We don't overwhelm you with action in these chapters, but we do ask you to make many small adjustments in your life that add up to significant change over time.

For all intents and purposes, this is a book of advice. As minimalists, we start with the material possessions, and then, once we've cleared the excess, we move beyond the stuff to the most important aspects of life: health, relationships, passions, growth, and contribution. These Five Values are the fundaments of living a meaningful life.

Finally, it is important to note that while we are sharing our sixty combined years of living through these pages, we do not have all the answers. The strategies, experiments, and stories we share in this book are things we've learned from innumerable sources, from Elizabeth Gilbert to Tony Robbins and everyone in between. The common thread, however, is that these are the strategies that have worked well for us and thousands of other people. Although we're all different, we're all looking for the same thing: how to live with more meaning.

CHAPTER 1: OUR ARRIVAL

Are You Happy?

The material possessions we accumulate will not make us happy. We all know this, and yet we often search for life's meaning through accumulating more possessions. Real happiness, however, comes from who we are—from who we've become. Real happiness comes from within. Likewise, discontentment is also a result of who we've become.

If you want to base your life on that of the average person, then this book is not for you—because the average person is not happy. And just because most people are unhappy doesn't mean you must be unhappy, too. You needn't settle for a mediocre life just because the people around you did.

Of course, *happiness* is not the point—a meaningful life is. We must stop searching for happiness and instead start looking for *meaning*. If our short-term actions align with our long-term values, we'll find purpose in whatever we're doing. Paradoxically, it is this way of living—living *deliberately*—that leads to true happiness. Not ephemeral or fleeting happiness, but lasting contentment that is reinforced by a life of discipline, attention, awareness, and intentionality. Happiness is merely a byproduct.

Finding Discontent

In 2009, life looked great for both of us. We both worked for the same telecommunications corporation (Joshua since 1999, Ryan since 2004); we both enjoyed the perks of a lifestyle most people envied; we both lived our version of the American Dream. But for some reason neither one of us could explain at the time, we were not happy, we didn't feel fulfilled, and we certainly didn't feel content.

The topic of happiness began peeking its head into our conversations more frequently as time passed. With each promotion at work, with each award or fancy trip we won, with every nugget of praise we received, the happiness accompanying those things quickly came and went. The faster it came, the faster it left. So we sought happiness by attempting to get more of these nuggets of praise, trying to improve our feelings of self-worth and significance by "achieving" more. We worked harder and harder to obtain these affirmations of worth, often working twice as many hours as the average American to prove our value.

It was something like a cocaine high. The more praise we received, the more we needed it to function, the more we needed it to feel happy. It got to the point where we were living just to break even emotionally.

Discontent flooded our lives. We knew something needed to change, but we weren't sure what. So we did what most Americans do: we tried to purchase happiness. Even though we were both earning more than six figures in well-respected positions, we spent more money than we made, purchasing things like luxury cars, large houses, big-screen TVs, fancy furniture, expensive vacations, and everything else our heavily mediated consumer culture told us would make us happy.

But it didn't make us happy. It brought us more depression and discontent, because not only did the old feelings stick around, but we piled on to those feelings by going into debt. And when the temporary high from each of our purchases dissipated, we were left feeling depressed, empty, alone, and helpless.

Then, in late 2009, a series of alarming events made Joshua begin to question every aspect of his life, including his material possessions, his career, his success, and the meaning of life.

A Slow Burn

But let's rewind our story a bit, because our discontent didn't suddenly descend from the heavens, striking us like a bolt of lightning. We didn't wake up one morning and say, *Gee, everything was fine yesterday, but today I'm unhappy.* Discontentment doesn't work that way. Rather, it's a slow burn; it's a pernicious problem that creeps into your life after years of subtle dissatisfaction.

It Started When We Were Young

The first signs of discontent appeared in our lives well before our days in corporate America: it started when we were children.

The two of us met twenty years ago in the fifth grade. We were ten years old, living near Dayton, Ohio, and even by then our lives were filled with discontent. We both grew up in dysfunctional households during the 1980s (before *dysfunctional* was a common term). Both sets of our parents were divorced. Joshua's parents separated when he was three; his mother succumbed to alcoholism, forcing him to raise himself most years after age six; his bipolar, schizophrenic father died when he was nine. Ryan's mother had similar substance-abuse issues, which later led to substance abuse for Ryan as a young adult. Both of us were raised in less than ideal conditions for much of our childhoods, which in retrospect was a recipe for disaster.

By age twelve, we were both overweight, uncool, and utterly unhappy with our lives. We did things to try to escape. Back then, the easiest escape was food. We experienced instant gratification by stuffing our faces; we felt certain we would be happy, at least for a moment. Food was one of the few aspects of our lives we could control, because everything else felt so out of control. We lived in dilapidated, cockroach-infested apartments with single mothers who cared about us, but who were more concerned with getting drunk or high than providing for their children.

As we approached high school, Ryan moved into his father's home—a much stabler household. His father owned a small wallpapering company and was able to provide a better lower-middle-class lifestyle. Ryan's father was the antithesis of his mother: he held a stable job, he showed he cared in myriad ways, and he was a devout Jehovah's Witness. The long list of positive changes was too much for Ryan to handle all at once, so while he did his best to conform to the strict household rules, he also rebelled, experimenting with alcohol, marijuana, and harder drugs.

Joshua took a different route. While he didn't indulge in alcohol or drugs—because he was so turned off by his mother's rampant alcoholism—he found another way to cope: namely, obsession and compulsion in the form of OCD. He discovered that even though he couldn't control his living situation—the tumbledown apartment, the drunken mother, the lack of money —he could control himself. So he lost a lot of weight during his freshman year in high school, in an unhealthy way (by eating very little), and he spent hours organizing his meager possessions, obsessing over the smallest things, searching for some kind of order in a world of chaos.

During our last year of high school, in 1998, we had a memorable conversation that unknowingly became the tipping point that led us into the chaos and confusion of consumerism. Because we grew up relatively poor, we thought the key to our happiness would be money; specifically: *If we could just make $50,000 a year, then we'd be set.* Our parents hadn't earned that kind of money, and they weren't happy, so we figured if we could pass an arbitrary threshold ($50,000 in this case), then we would somehow be happy. It sounds ridiculous now, but it made perfect sense to a couple eighteen-year-olds about to enter the world on their own.

We graduated high school in 1999, and we went in separate directions for a few years. Neither of us went to college straightaway; instead, we both entered the working world.

Ryan worked for his father, hanging wallpaper and painting walls in opulent houses throughout southwest Ohio. Joshua found a sales job with a large corporation. Both careers were steeped in certain monetary expectations. Neither of us particularly enjoyed what we were doing, but we didn't know any better—we didn't realize you could actually do work you enjoyed. For us, our jobs were designed to do two things for our lifestyle: allow us to make money, and give us a certain kind of social status.

Ryan was making enough money to live. It wasn't great money, but it paid the bills. He also earned an identity from his job. A fleet of half-a-dozen paint trucks, "Nicodemus" plastered on the side of each, patrolled the streets of Warren County, Ohio, silently speaking volumes about his future. There was comfort in knowing that one day he would take over his father's business, making it his own, and maybe even passing it on to his future children.

But Ryan also knew the painting business wouldn't make him rich. He was painting multi-million-dollar homes, which he knew he'd never afford himself, even when he took over his dad's business, which, if he worked really hard, he'd do once his dad retired in a decade or two. There was a fair amount of discontent that showed up for Ryan, realizing he would never be able to get something he wanted. At the time he didn't know why he wanted a palatial home or why it would make him happy; he was merely unhappy that he would never afford such luxuries. So Ryan searched for contentment in other ways.

Joshua found a job at which he had the potential to earn more money than the people with whom he went to high school, a job that had long-term career-growth possibilities. All he had to do was work like a sled dog to "get results." So work like a dog he did, often working more than a month straight—seven days a week—without a day off. The more he worked, the more he sold. And the more he sold, the more money he earned, and the more he was showered with praise. At eighteen he was already making more money than his mother ever had. He was poised for (corporate) greatness. At least ostensibly.

But Joshua experienced discontent, too. Although he was making more than $50,000 by nineteen, he had little personal time. The corporate world of "performing" and "achieving" was taking its toll, so he tried to purchase happiness, attempting to manufacture a life of contentment.

Manufactured Contentment

Unhappy with our jobs and our lives, we tried to fix our discontent in different ways.

Ryan turned to a few extremes. First, he turned back to his father's religion—the religion of his childhood—swearing off drugs and worldly activities, becoming a devout Jehovah's Witness, embracing its tenets and searching for life's meaning through religion. Ryan married his high school girlfriend at eighteen, a few months after graduating high school. He and his wife adopted the JW lifestyle, got a mortgage for a small house in the hometown in which they were raised, and started talking about creating a family together.

But it became a marriage saturated with fear and distrust. After three years of tedious matrimony, the marriage ended nastily, upon which Ryan turned back to drugs and alcohol, searching for an escape from his painful failed reality.

Joshua, on the other hand, continued his laser-focused work in corporate America, consistently performing as one of the best sales people in the company. He earned his first promotion to a leadership position at 22, making him the youngest person in the company's 130-year history to have earned the position.

With this promotion came more money, more responsibility, and even more work. Joshua's life was consumed by work. At 23, he got married, built a large house in suburbia, and continued to work more and more as his personal life passed by in the unfocused background. He hardly realized he had gotten married. He neglected and took for granted the relationship with his wife. He hardly spent time in their large house, which contained more bedrooms than inhabitants. Above all, he avoided the discontent brewing within him. He knew he wasn't happy, but he'd get there one day, right? And so life went on at its breakneck pace.

To deal with his more subtle discontent, Joshua tried to buy his happiness. He spent money on *stuff*, buying fancy clothes, expensive vacations, consumer electronics, multitudes of unnecessary junk. When those things didn't bring lasting happiness, he turned to his childhood vice of food. By his early twenties, he weighed more than ever: he was 70 pounds overweight and severely out of shape. *But at least I'm making money!* he thought, giving himself an identity in his career, a kind of status and satisfaction in knowing he performed well at his job, albeit a job he wasn't passionate about.

Reconnecting the Duo

It was around this time that we reconnected, almost accidentally, at the nadir of our early twenties.

Ryan decided that taking over his father's business was not for him. He didn't know what he wanted to do with his life, but he figured he'd give the corporate world a shot. Because if he could just make over $50,000 a year, then life would be good and he would be happy, right?

So, in 2004, shortly after Joshua got married and Ryan got divorced, Joshua hired Ryan to work at the corporation at which he had slaved for the last half-decade. Like Joshua, Ryan quickly excelled, working exceptionally hard, becoming one of the company's top-performing salespeople.

We both earned several more promotions over the years, during our mid- and late-twenties—promotions with fancy titles like *Channel Manager*, *Regional Manager*, and *Director*. And with those titles came more money and more responsibility and more work. Sadly, far darker things came with those promotions, as well: anxiety and stress and worry and overwhelm and depression.

And yet, try as we did, our search for happiness through status and material possessions never yielded real, lasting happiness or contentment.

By our late twenties we were earning great money at jobs we disliked, but we were in debt—financially and emotionally.

Back to the Future

Fast-forward back to 2009, back to our 80-hour workweeks, back to our ostensibly perfect lives that were crumbling on the inside.

On October 8, 2009, Joshua's mother died of stage-four lung cancer. She battled it over a year, enduring repeat chemo and radiation treatments. But as the cancer spread to her brain and other organs, she was no match for the disease in the end.

Oddly enough, the cancer seemed to be a metaphor for Joshua's life. While things looked good on the surface—the marriage, the fancy job, the cars, the trinkets of success—there was something seriously wrong on the inside.

Neither of us was happy. When we told ourselves a decade earlier we'd be happy if we could just make $50,000 per year, we were wrong. At first, in our early twenties, we thought maybe we had simply miscalculated the exact amount required to be happy, so we changed our estimation: If we could make $60,000 per year, then we could be happy, right? And when that didn't work: If we could make $75,000 and then $90,000 and then $100,000 per year, then we could be happy, right? It was a never-ending cycle. Each year we made more money, and each year we spent more than we earned in an effort to subdue our perpetual discontent created by the lifestyles we were living. The equation itself was broken.

A week after Joshua's mother died, we had another conversation about happiness. We discussed why we weren't happy and what it would take to make us happy. Obviously the old formula of *If we could make $X, then we could be happy* was not panning out. We were both making over six figures, we were both successful 28-year-old young executives, and we both "had it figured out" according to cultural standards. But we didn't have it figured out at all.

Was this what we had been waiting for our entire lives? Were we going to continue to work ridiculously long hours at a corporation that didn't care about us? Were we going to work our way into upper-management—becoming COOs or CEOs with seven- or even eight-figure salaries—just to be even more depressed by the time we were in our forties? It didn't sound appealing to us: our dreams of climbing the corporate ladder seemed more like nightmares the more we talked about it.

The death of Joshua's mother put everything into perspective: We have only a finite amount of time on this earth. It can be spent accumulating monetary wealth, or it can be spent in a meaningful way—the latter of which doesn't necessarily preclude someone from the former, but the relentless pursuit of riches doesn't lead to a meaningful life.

So we decided to take an inventory of our lives. We wanted to find out what was making us unhappy, and what we needed to do to change those things in our lives, so we could experience happiness, passion, freedom.

Anchors

First, we identified our *anchors*. We had discovered "getting what we wanted" (large houses, bigger paychecks, material possessions, and corporate awards) wasn't making us happy, so we wanted to identify what was anchoring us—what was making us feel stuck and preventing us from growing.

The concept of anchors struck a chord with both of us. It forced us to take an honest look in the mirror and identify everything we thought might be holding us back from living happy, fulfilled lives.

The exercise we performed was simple: over the course of one week, each of us wrote down anything we thought might be an anchor (the first step to solving a problem is to identify the problem, right?). As the week progressed, our lists of anchors grew, and by the end of the week Joshua had counted 83 anchors and Ryan, 54. Plenty of anchors.

Our next step was to identify our priorities. We started prioritizing by dividing our anchors into two categories: major anchors and minor anchors.

Major anchors were the most obvious things keeping us from feeling free, including our houses (namely the large mortgage payments that went with them), certain relationships with people (namely unhealthy relationships that didn't add value to our lives), car payments and other large bills, major debts, our careers, and anything else that demanded an inordinate amount of time without returning commensurate value to our lives.

Minor anchors made up the bulk of our lists and included cable bills, Internet bills, other bills, smaller debts, unused clothes, unused household items, household clutter, certain unproductive peripheral relationships, daily drive time, and other small things that consumed small amounts of our time, attention, and focus.

We decided that ridding ourselves of many of these anchors over a period of time would let us reclaim much of our own time, which could then be spent in more meaningful ways. Because the major anchors appeared to be the hardest to tackle, we started with those first. For example, every extra penny Joshua earned was spent on making extra payments toward his debts. No more trips, vacations, or fancy dinners; all his money went toward paying off his car and his vast credit card debt, which, despite a healthy income, had climbed to an unbelievable level—greater than six figures. Eventually, over a two-year period, we paid off our cars and paid down our debts. Other major anchors were addressed in a similar fashion. We eventually jettisoned many of our possessions, eliminating the excess in favor of things we liked and enjoyed—things we actually used in our daily lives. Over the course of two years, our anchors of old were no longer weighing us down.

Making Difficult Decisions

Because some of the major anchors involved our relationships with other people, some tough decisions had to be made. Soon after Joshua's mother died, Joshua decided his marriage of nearly six years wasn't working. He knew that neither he nor his wife was happy, that neither of their values or desires were aligned, and that they both wanted vastly different things from life. They loved each other and wanted to find a way to make their marriage work, so they sat down and discussed their differences and worked on a plan to save their marriage. They attended marriage counseling and took steps to come into better alignment, working together for months in an effort to repair a broken marriage. Their differences, however, were too great, so Joshua and his wife decided to part ways. It was the hardest decision he ever had to make. Thankfully, as time passed, they were able to remain close friends who still care about each other deeply.

Furthermore, Joshua was faced with the dilemma of what to do with his mother's stuff after her death—what to do with those sentimental items we tend to hold on to in perpetuity. His mother had lived a thousand miles away, in Florida; and, after she passed, it was his responsibility to vacate her small, one-bedroom apartment, brimming with belongings. His mother had an interior decorator's good taste, so none of her stuff was "junk" in the *Hoarders* sense of the word, which made letting go of anything difficult. Nevertheless, there was a lot of stuff in her home, likely three or more apartments' worth in her tiny dwelling, so he knew some things would have to go.

His mom had lived her life as a constant shopper, always accumulating more stuff. She had antique furniture throughout her apartment, a stunning oak canopy-bed that consumed almost her entire bedroom, two closets bulging with clothes, picture frames standing on every flat surface, original artwork hanging on the walls, and creative decorations in every nook and cranny and crevasse—64 years of accumulations.

So Joshua did what any son would do: He rented a large U-

Haul truck. Then he called a storage facility back in Ohio to make sure they had a big enough storage unit. The truck was $1,600; the storage facility was $120 per month. Financially the cost was expensive, but he quickly discovered the emotional cost was much higher.

At first Joshua didn't want to let go of anything. If you've lost a loved one, or you've been through a similarly emotional time, then you understand exactly how hard it was for him to let go of any of those possessions. So instead of letting go, he planned to cram every trinket and figurine and piece of oversized furniture into that tiny storage locker in Ohio. Floor to ceiling. That way he knew Mom's stuff was there if he ever wanted it, if he ever needed access to it for some incomprehensible reason. Just in case.

The week after her death, Joshua began boxing up her belongings: Every picture frame, every porcelain doll, every doily on every shelf. He packed every bit of her that remained.

Or so he thought.

Then he looked under her bed.

Among the organized chaos that comprised the crawlspace beneath her bed, there were four boxes, each labeled with a number: 1, 2, 3, 4. Each numbered box was sealed with packing tape. Joshua cut through the tape and found old papers from his elementary school days—grades 1–4. Spelling tests, cursive writing lessons, artwork—it was all there, every shred of paper from his first four years of school. It was evident she hadn't accessed the sealed boxes in years, and yet she had held on to these things because she was trying to hold on to pieces of her son, pieces of the past, much like Joshua was attempting to hold on to pieces of her and her past now.

That's when he realized his retention efforts were futile. He could hold on to her memories without her stuff, just as she had always remembered him and his childhood and all their memories without ever accessing those sealed boxes under her bed. She didn't need papers from twenty-five years ago to remember her son, just as her son didn't need a storage locker filled with her belongings to remember her.

So Joshua called U-Haul and canceled the truck. Then, over the next twelve days, he donated almost all her stuff to places and people who could actually use it. Of course it was difficult to let go, but Joshua learned several lessons during this experience:

We are not our stuff.
We are more than our possessions.
Our memories are within us, not our things.
Our stuff weighs on us mentally and emotionally.
Old photographs can be scanned.
You can take pictures of items you want to remember.
Items that are sentimental for us can be useful to others.
Letting go is freeing.

We don't think sentimental items are bad or evil or that holding on to them is wrong. Rather, we think the malign nature of sentimental items is far more subtle. If you want to get rid of an item but the only reason you are holding on to it is for sentimental reasons—if it's weighing on you, if it's an anchor— then perhaps it's time to get rid of it, perhaps it's time to free yourself of the weight. That doesn't mean you need to get rid of everything, though.

One by one, over time, the two of us tackled many of our

anchors—big and small. In the process of tackling our anchors, we searched for ways to do so more efficiently. We searched for examples of people who had overcome their fears, who had freed themselves of their anchors and started living more meaningful lives. This is how we stumbled upon the concepts of minimalism.

Discovering Minimalism

In late 2009, shortly after Joshua's mother had died, while his marriage was in shambles and we were both unhappy with our current nose-to-the-grindstone situations, Joshua came across a website called *Exile Lifestyle*, developed by a guy named Colin Wright.

We were intrigued by Colin's website. Here was this young, 24-year-old entrepreneur living an amazing life—a seemingly impossible life. He'd left his high-paying career to pursue his passions—traveling the world and running his businesses from anywhere. His website—what he called a *blog*, a term we were unfamiliar with at the time—documented his travels and allowed his thousands of readers to participate in his journey: Colin's readers vote on where he will travel next.

We were amazed that this guy "left everything" to travel to a new country every four months—not that we wanted to travel that extensively ourselves (we didn't), but we did want to have the freedom to pursue our own passions, which we discovered weren't inside the corporate juggernaut.

Colin also used a term with which we were utterly unfamiliar: he said he was a *minimalist*. On his website he wrote about how this movement called *minimalism* allowed him to focus on the important stuff in his life, while shedding the excess junk that had gotten in the way. This was fascinating: it was like someone turned on the lightbulb for us for the first time and presented us with a tool to help us weed through the clutter in our lives to finally get to what was important. Because he traveled, Colin owned only 72 things at the time—there were pictures of all his possessions on his website—and all of his possessions fit into a bag he carried with him while he traveled. The most striking part about this story was Colin's contentment: He exuded happiness and excitement and passion. He loved his life.

Although we deeply respect Colin, we didn't want to live like him—we didn't want to travel the world or live with fewer than 100 things. But we did want the freedom that his minimalist lifestyle afforded him, and we wanted the happiness and passion that accompanied that freedom. So, during the first half of 2010, we slowly removed our anchors, one by one, as we followed Colin's journey.

But, at 30, maybe we were too old and too rooted to become minimalists. Maybe this minimalism thing was only for young guys without many possessions who wanted to travel extensively.

We discovered that wasn't true, either.

Through Colin we discovered two other minimalists who were in many ways much like us: Leo Babauta and Joshua Becker.

Leo Babauta, creator of the website *Zen Habits*, had a story that resonated with us immediately. He was a once-divorced man in his mid-thirties who overcame scads of adversity to live more meaningfully. Using minimalism to simplify his life, he had accomplished some amazing feats in just a few years: he quit smoking, lost 70 pounds, gotten into the best shape of his life, climbed out of debt, moved from Guam to San Francisco, and quit his corporate job but was still able to provide for his wife and six children.

Similarly, thirty-something Joshua Becker, a husband and father of two living in Vermont, simplified his suburban-family life using minimalism while maintaining his job at a local church and helping other people learn more about minimalism through his website, *Becoming Minimalist.*

Leo Babauta and Joshua Becker proved to us minimalism wasn't only for single guys who didn't want to work a nine-to-five: it was for anyone interested in living a simpler, more intentional life. It was for anyone who wanted to focus on the important aspects in life, rather than the material possessions so heavily linked to success and happiness by our culture.

In fact, on our website we have a page dedicated to defining minimalism in a tongue-in-cheek way, poking fun at the cynics and skeptics who treat minimalism as a trend or fad. We start our definition with:

To be a minimalist you must live with fewer than 100 things, and you can't own a car or a home or a TV, and you can't have a career, and you have to be able to live in exotic places all over the world, and you have to write a blog, and you can't have children, and you have to be a young white male from a privileged background.

Okay, we're joking. Obviously. But people who dismiss minimalism as a fad usually mention some of the above "restrictions" as to why they could "never be a minimalist."

The truth is minimalism isn't about any of those things, but it can help you accomplish almost all that stuff if you're so inclined.

If you desire to live with fewer than 100 things or not own a car or travel all over the world, minimalism can help.

But that's not the point.

The point is minimalism is a tool to help you achieve freedom. Freedom from fear, freedom from worry, freedom from overwhelm, freedom from guilt, freedom from depression, freedom from enslavement. Freedom. Real freedom.

A minimalist can, however, own a car and a house and have children and a career. Minimalism looks different for everyone because it's about finding what is essential to *you*. There are tons of successful minimalists who do some or all of these things (see minimalists.com/links for a list of minimalists). So how can they all be so different and yet still be minimalists? That brings us back to our original question: *What is minimalism?*

Minimalism is a tool we use to live a meaningful life. There are no rules. Rather, minimalism is simply about stripping away the unnecessary things in your life so you can focus on what's important. Ultimately, minimalism is the thing that gets us past the things so we can focus on life's most important things— which actually aren't things at all.

Minimalism has helped us in several ways, including:

Reclaiming our time
Ridding ourselves of excess stuff
Enjoying our lives
Discovering meaning in our lives
Living in the moment
Focusing on what's important

Pursuing our passions
Finding happiness
Doing anything we want to do
Finding our missions
Experiencing freedom
Creating more, consuming less

How has minimalism helped us with these things? Minimalism is a lifestyle choice. Minimalists choose to get rid of the unnecessary in favor of what's important. But the level of specificity is up to you. Minimalists search for happiness not through things, but through life itself; thus, it's up to you to determine what is necessary and what is superfluous to your life. Throughout this book we will give you some ideas of how to determine these things and how to achieve a minimalist lifestyle without succumbing to a strict code or a set of rules.

A word of warning: It isn't easy to take the first few steps, but the journey gets much easier and more rewarding the further you go. But the first steps into minimalism often take radical changes in mindset, actions, and habits.

So, if we had to sum it up in one sentence, we would say, *Minimalism is a tool to eliminate life's excess, focus on the essentials, and find happiness, fulfillment, and freedom.*

Embracing Minimalism

It was as our lives were spiraling downward in ever-diminishing circles toward oblivion that we embraced minimalism. It was a beacon in the night. We feverishly scoured Internet page after Internet page looking for more information and guidance and enlightenment, watching and learning and trying to understand what this whole minimalism thing was about. Through months of research (while we removed our anchors) we traveled further and further down the rabbit hole, and over time we discovered a group of people without a lot of things but with myriad happiness and passion and freedom, things for which we desperately yearned.

Eventually we embraced these concepts—the concepts of minimalism and simplicity—as a way of life, and we discovered we, too, could be happy, but it wasn't through owning more stuff; it wasn't through accumulation. We took back control of our lives so we could focus on what's important, so we could focus on life's deeper meaning.

Happiness, as far as we are concerned, is achieved internally through living a meaningful life, a life that is filled with passion and freedom, a life in which we can grow and contribute to others in meaningful ways. These are the bedrocks of happiness. Not stuff.

Creating "The Minimalists"

In the summer of 2010 we had no intentions of writing nonfiction online or starting a website about minimalism. But then, almost accidentally, Joshua met Colin Wright in person while on a trip to New York City in June. Meeting Colin solidified his online persona: his personality shone through in person, displaying layers of happiness and contentment that didn't seem possible to a discontented man approaching 30, living on the corporate continuum.

They met in Manhattan after connecting on Twitter. Joshua had been writing fiction throughout his twenties, whenever he had a free moment outside of work. He knew Colin earned a living online by publishing his own material, so he wanted to pick Colin's brain about self-publishing. When they met for lunch, Colin encouraged Joshua to explore the nontraditional route of publishing his fiction, citing several resources that would later become helpful (see asymmetrical.co/how-to for a list of resources). They stayed in contact after that initial meeting and eventually worked on several projects together, including Colin's memoir, *My Exile Lifestyle*, and Joshua's novel, *As a Decade Fades*.

During that meeting, Colin said one thing that stuck with Joshua—the one thing that led him to team up with Ryan to create *The Minimalists*:

You should do something online. You could make a difference. The world needs people like you to help them see things clearly.

Joshua wrote those words in his journal. They stuck with him long after the meeting. And with those words we decided to create *The Minimalists*. We wanted to do two things with our website: we wanted to document our personal journeys into minimalism, and we wanted to help other people live more meaningful lives using minimalism as a foundation. We started building the site in November 2010, and quickly discovered we were clueless about how to create a website. We didn't know the first thing about HTML or *blogging* or writing nonfiction online (sure, Joshua had his fiction-writing experience, which helped with our writing, but we were clueless about the rest). So we did extensive research and built our site over a six-week timeframe, laboring vigorously until the last minute (for an in-depth look at how we created our website, read our essay, "How to Start a

Successful Blog," at minimalists.com/blog). We officially launched *TheMinimalists.com* on December 14, 2010.

And so there we were: two suit-and-tie corporate guys, taking advice from some millennial blogger. We had started a website, documented our entire journey into minimalism, and started writing a few essays a week for the site.

Then several months of unexpected excitement transpired, and our lives changed within nine months of creating our website. We met some of the most amazing people on the Internet, eventually turning those online relationships into real-life friendships, including the aforementioned Leo Babauta and Joshua Becker, as well as myriad others, among them Julien Smith, Chris Guillebeau, and Courtney Carver. With the help of many of these outstanding folks, as well as our small number of initial readers relentlessly sharing our essays, our website grew exponentially—within nine months we had over 100,000 monthly readers. By that time people were spending over 11,000 hours on our site each month. We had been featured on popular websites all over the Web. We received the most incredible emails about how we changed people's lives with our essays. As a consequence, we both left our corporate jobs and began focusing full-time on living more meaningful lives. (To read more about our exit from the corporate world, read chapter seven of our memoir, *Everything That Remains*, or Joshua's essay, "Why I Walked Away from My Six-Figure Career," at minimalists.com/quit.)

What It Means to Live a Meaningful Life

What does it mean to live a meaningful life? Generally, through our essays and books, we speak of minimalism as a tool that has allowed us to pursue more meaningful lives, so it's important we define what this means.

After much cerebration, deliberation, discussion, research, and experimentation, we discovered Five Values that allow us to live a meaningful life:

1. Health
2. Relationships
3. Passions
4. Growth
5. Contribution

It took us months of removing the anchors from our lives, and getting rid of the clutter that surrounded us, to uncover these Five Values. We didn't stumble into them, though; instead, we discovered what was most important in our lives through trial and error.

Minimalism made this discovery possible. By 28, everything in our lives seemed foggy. We had everything we were *supposed* to have, everything our culture advertised would make us happy, and yet we weren't. Worse, we had reached the point at which we didn't know what was important anymore. Getting rid of the clutter in our lives allowed us to rediscover these five key areas. Thus, getting rid of our stuff was the initial bite at the apple, allowing us to make room to fill our lives with more meaningful pursuits.

Through months of rigorous documentation, the Five Values are the areas we changed in our lives that had the largest positive effect and resulted in more satisfaction and contentment for the two of us. The following five chapters discuss each of these concepts in depth, much more so than can be discussed on our website. Throughout these chapters we consider why these Five Values are the most important areas of our lives and how minimalism has allowed us to focus on these values, citing personal examples of how we changed our lives in all five areas.

The book's final chapter, "Confluence," binds together these Five Values and asks the reader some important questions about their life. These questions are not rhetorical; they are meant to make you think, take notes, and make lists based on those questions. Similarly, as we stated in this book's foreword, we encourage you to actively engage in all the chapters by reading the content more than once, writing notes in the margins, highlighting meaningful passages, making your own lists, and, most important, taking action.

Ultimately, this book is meant to make you take little actions each day that will radically improve your life over time.

Let's begin, shall we?

CHAPTER 2: HEALTH

The Importance of Health

Health is the most important of the Five Values. Don't believe us? Let us prove it.

Imagine winning the lottery, finding a perfect match in your significant other, paying off your debts, moving into your dream home (on the beach, of course), and not needing to work another day in your life.

Now imagine you wake up tomorrow morning with a sharp pain in your gut. You leave your beach house, drive to the doctor's office in your luxury vehicle, and wait for her to tell you what's wrong. "You have less than a month to live," she says. "And you likely won't be able to do much more than get out of bed after today." Oh, the heartache. You finally got "everything you ever wanted," but your failing health immediately took it away, and your possessions couldn't do a thing for you. Without your health you're unable to enjoy even the simplest things in life.

Defining Health

We are not health experts. This is not a book about diet and exercise, and by the end of this chapter it might start to feel like one, but we assure you that is not our intent. Rather, we believe your health is the best place to start your journey toward a more meaningful life. We want you to enjoy your life, and living a healthy lifestyle gives you the optimum conditions to do so. Everything in this chapter is based on our personal experiences of weight loss, exercise, dietary changes, and lifestyle changes that have helped us and others live more meaningful lives.

For the purposes of this book, we are referring to *physical* health when we use the general term *health*, although we recognize *health* extends beyond the physical realm: *emotional* health, *mental* health, *spiritual* health, and *financial* health are all broad concepts that are important aspects of enriching your life. While these concepts aren't touched upon directly within the pages of this book, we discuss them in great detail on our website (see minimalists.com/understanding [emotional health], minimalists.com/dan [mental health], minimalists.com/sam [spiritual health], and minimalists.com/freedom [financial health] for in-depth discussions on each topic).

Health Is Not a Destination

We often have a misguided, binary view of physical health. Case in point: a reader took umbrage with a "sign" in our essay, "11 Signs You Might Be Broke" (minimalists.com/broke). She didn't like what we had written about health, stating, "I'm normally a huge fan [of The Minimalists,] but this article really annoyed me just because … [it] came across quite judgmental of sick people. … The article might have been better if they'd stuck to ten points."

But, dear reader, health is the most important aspect of the whole article! Without health we have nothing. Although of course "health" is a continuum: it is different for each of us. Personal health is, by definition, personal.

The statement in the essay—"Unhealthy equals depression"— does not suggest we should compare our personal health with everyone else's (comparison is often unhealthy and should be avoided), and it certainly is not a judgment of anyone who's sick. Rather, we all want to be in the best possible health given our unique circumstances.

For example, Joshua broke his back while playing basketball in the eighth grade, two decades ago, and still has a broken vertebra today, which, besides being painful, significantly limits his range of motion compared to, say, a gymnast or an athlete or just your average 30-something-year-old guy. He can hardly tie his shoes sometimes.

However, that doesn't mean Joshua shouldn't strive to be as healthy as he can be given his constraints. In this sense, health is perspectival, and so if we want to be happy, then we all must strive to be the healthiest versions of ourselves—broken bones, sickness, warts and all. In fact, the Internet is filled with shining examples of people with diseases, disabilities, and broken backs living meaningful lives because they live as healthily as they can according to their individual situations.

It's also worth noting that when we talk about health, we're not talking about vanity muscles or improved statistics or competing with others. Those are end results, destinations. But health is not a destination; it is a vehicle.

So, okay, maybe Joshua will never make it to the NBA with his bad back (not to mention his mediocre ball-handling skills), but that doesn't mean he should feel defeated, broke, broken. No, it means he must take care of the vehicle he has, providing it with regular tune-ups (daily stretching, regular exercise, and occasional chiropractor visits, as well as a good diet, adequate sleep, and daily meditation), which will help him better enjoy the journey ahead.

The Main Ingredients

In its simplest terms, there are two main ingredients of living a healthy life: *eating* and *exercising*. In other words: what we *put into* our bodies and what we *do with* our bodies.

This might sound overly simplistic—at the surface it is simple—but, fundamentally, the two things that most impact your physical health are what you eat and how you exercise. You already know this, at least intellectually, but this chapter is designed to help you feel it emotionally, and to provide you with simple tools to help you improve your health.

Feeling Better

The desire to improve your health has little to do with *looking better*. That's not what we're concerned with when we talk about *getting healthy* or *living a healthy life* (although, nearly 100% of the time, a person who starts living a healthier lifestyle starts looking better almost immediately, which is a fantastic bonus). Instead, we're far more concerned about how you *feel*. We want you to *feel better*; *looking better* is a nice perk that is essentially guaranteed once you start feeling better.

Thus, we're not concerned with social-media-worthy muscles in these pages; rather, we're concerned with how you feel. We know if you feel better, you'll better enjoy every other facet of your life.

What You Put into Your Body

Please note that we use the term *diet* throughout the next few sections to describe a *dietary lifestyle* (i.e., a change in what you consume on a daily basis). We do not, however, use the word *diet* to describe a temporary prescribed set of planned meals that will get you to a specific weight-loss goal (e.g., lose 30 pounds in 30 days).

A change in dietary lifestyle is not only a change in what you consume, but a change in how you *think about* what you consume. A temporary *diet* almost always fails after the post-*diet* behavior commences. A lifestyle change, by definition, can't fail unless you make a negative change thereafter.

It's also important to note that there is not a singular, ideal dietary model to follow to live a healthier life. This frustrates some people because it is much easier to be told what to eat; it's much easier to follow a strict set of guidelines from which you are not allowed to deviate.

Our focus in the next few sections is on food (followed by several sections about exercise), but the above section title is deliberately broader than just food because *what you put into your body* encompasses more than your diet. It's important to be cognizant of anything that goes into your body—anything you ingest, like food or medicine, as well as anything that enters your body in any other way (e.g., through the skin).

Remember, the desire here isn't to lose weight or look better; the desire is to live a healthier life and feel better.

Foods to Avoid

With respect to the foods you eat, and irrespective of your dietary needs or requirements, there are certain foods you should completely eliminate from your diet if you want to feel better.

Processed and packaged foods. Our food should be as close to its original state as possible. The additives and preservatives in packaged foods add no nutritional value to your diet, and the chemicals in some of these foods can be harmful to your long-term health.

Sugar. This includes all varieties of plain sugar (cane, raw, etc.), as well as anything referred to as *sweets* (cola, cake, candy, etc.).

Drastically Reduce or Eliminate

This part is usually the hardest part for people to follow, because it's easier to fast than to diet. Consequently, it's easier to eliminate certain foods from your diet completely (*I'm not allowed to eat this!*) than it is to reduce the consumption of an item (*Oh, one more bowl of pasta won't kill me!*). That kind of mentality makes reduction a slippery slope, one that often leads back to regular consumption. We recognize that eliminating all the following items from your diet might not be ideal, but you can always eliminate them for just ten days (you can do anything for ten days, right?) and reintroduce small amounts if you must.

Gluten, breads, and pastas. Many people are allergic or sensitive to gluten without even knowing it. In 2008, Joshua discovered he was allergic to gluten after experiencing several stomach issues that gradually got worse. His doctor informed him he was allergic to gluten, and, once he eliminated it from his diet, he noticed a remarkable difference in the way he felt. Furthermore, breads and pastas (even the rare, gluten-free varieties) add unnecessary carbohydrates and sugars to your diet, which cause you to gain weight. Breads and pastas are processed foods that our bodies often have a difficult time digesting. The two of us tend to eat small amounts of rice instead of these foods.

Any drinks other than water. Coffee, caffeinated tea, soda, bottled juice, et cetera—none of these liquids are water. Most add unnecessary calories to your diet, and they will never hydrate you like water.

Dairy. You don't have to be a vegan to live a healthy life. In fact, both of us consume small amounts of dairy occasionally (although we've drastically reduced our consumption). But ask yourself: Why are humans the only animals who consume another animal's breast milk? Do you think the human digestive system is designed to digest a cow's milk? Can you remove dairy from your diet for ten days and notice a difference?

Meat. This one is controversial. We stopped eating meat as an experiment a few years ago and noticed phenomenal results, so we never went back (other than fish, which we discuss in the following sections). The best advice we can give you is to test it yourself—

stop eating meat for at least ten days and notice the difference it makes. Then decide for yourself.

Incorporate More

We replaced the foods we reduced or eliminated with healthier alternatives we enjoy.

Water. We recommend drinking at least half your bodyweight in ounces of water every day. If you weigh 200 pounds, drink at least 100 ounces of water.

Green drinks. Want a boost in your energy? Not getting your daily veggies? Drink a green drink. We like Amazing Grass Green Superfood, which contains a large chunk of the vitamins and nutrients you need every day. Just mix a tablespoon or two with ten ounces of water, drink it, and feel the difference. We drink at least two every day. You'll notice a difference in energy and vitality immediately. Green drink also helps you fend off hunger, keeping you from overeating.

Fresh smoothies. Get yourself a NutriBullet and use it daily. A powerful blender is a great way to add copious amounts of kale, spinach, and other nutrient-dense greens into your diet. Can't afford a good blender? Sell your junk and buy one: we're certain the juicer will add more value to your life than your unused trinkets.

Vegetables. Vegetables are low in calories and high in essential vitamins and nutrients. Eat as many non-starchy vegetables as you want—they're good for you.

Beans and legumes. Beans and legumes add healthy proteins and carbohydrates to your diet. They also help you feel full so you don't overeat.

Fruits. Fruits are tricky. They are healthy—filled with necessary vitamins, acids, and water—but they also contain natural sugar. Thus, a couple pieces of fruit each day can be a healthy alternative to sweets, but we also recommend reducing your fruit consumption if it is one of your primary sources of food.

Fish. Some fish, such as salmon, contain crucial omega-3 fatty acids, which have been scientifically proven to reduce the risk of coronary heart disease. Omega-3 fatty acids also help maintain healthy triglyceride levels. Plus, fish is a great source of protein. That said, we recommend avoiding certain bottom-feeders (shrimp, crab, lobster, etc.) because they are the garbage men of the sea, eating every dead thing that sinks to the bottom.

Organic foods. Organic foods are free of pesticides and other chemicals, so it makes sense to consume them when you can— the fewer chemicals you put in your body, the better.

Special Diets

Again, we're not asking you to live by a strict "diet." Nor do we subscribe to any one particular dietary lifestyle as the end-all/be-all. Rather, we believe different people have different dietary needs, thus we encourage you to experiment with different elements of your diet until you find the results you want (i.e., until you feel better, until you feel healthy). In addition to the above mentioned foods to avoid, reduce, eliminate, and incorporate, here are examples of five diets from which we've seen great results.

Vegetarianism. Most people are familiar with vegetarianism, though there is an entire continuum of vegetarianism. At its fundament, a vegetarian diet eschews meat, but might include other animal products, such as dairy and eggs.

Veganism. A vegan's diet doesn't include any animal products (meat, dairy, eggs, honey, etc.). We both experimented with a strict vegan diet for one year (it was a one-dollar bet between the two of us, and Ryan won), and the results were astounding: we felt more energy, Ryan lost a considerable amount of weight, Joshua maintained a healthy weight, and, most important, we both felt better. Since that experiment, we decided to incorporate some dairy, eggs, and fish back into our diets, which leads us to the next diet.

Pescatarianism. This is essentially the diet to which we both adhere currently. Pescatarians are vegetarians who eat fish. We also consume some dairy products, albeit significantly less than we used to.

Paleo. Although neither of us subscribe to this diet (because we don't eat meat), we have friends who have had significant results from some form of paleo or primal diet. The Paleo Diet mimics the types of foods most people on Earth ate prior to the Agricultural Revolution (a mere 500 generations ago). These foods (fresh fruits, vegetables, lean meats, and seafood) are high in the beneficial nutrients that promote good health. The Paleo

Diet is low in foods that frequently cause weight gain, cardiovascular disease, diabetes, and numerous other health problems (refined sugars and grains, dairy, trans fats, salt, high-glycemic carbohydrates, and processed foods). The Paleo Diet encourages dieters to replace dairy and grain products with fresh fruits and vegetables—foods more nutritious than whole grains or dairy products. For more information visit paleoplan.com.

Intermittent fasting. Intermittent fasting is a pattern of eating that alternates between periods of fasting (consuming only water) and non-fasting. For example, a person who intermittently fasts might not eat for sixteen hours per day and then eat two or three meals within an eight-hour window. Thus, any of the four above mentioned dietary lifestyles could apply to intermittent fasting. People who attempt this diet (even for ten days) typically see wonderful results. As we were editing the first edition of this book, Joshua started adhering to this diet and saw incredible results in about a week—less body fat, a flatter stomach, and more toned muscles. Martin Berkhan has achieved unbelievable results with intermittent fasting (including muscle-mass results far beyond the scope of this book). You can read more about intermittent fasting and see Martin Berkhan's story at leangains.com.

Developing Daily Food Habits

Most drastic dietary changes fail long-term because they are overwhelming, so people find them too hard to maintain. Instead of establishing a diet plan, we encourage you to change your diet for ten days at a time (anyone can change for ten days, right?). Experiment with the aforementioned dietary lifestyles (not diet *plans*), and adhere to the diet that is right for you. Your diet is not something you do; it is the way you live your life with respect to food consumption, which means it's also not something you "come off of" either. Your dietary lifestyle is a permanent change, not something you adopt temporarily.

Thus, your diet is marked by the daily habits by which you live. Once you adopt a healthy dietary lifestyle, you will feel better, and your body will thank you. Food should be treated as nutrition, not entertainment.

Medicine, Drugs, and Chemicals

Take a look at your medicine cabinet. What kind of medication do you take? How many pills per day? Why do you take it? Are there alternatives? If so, have you tested them for yourself? If the doctor prescribed you something, did you ask why? Did you ask for a second opinion?

Or worse: Do you smoke? Consume too much alcohol? Use drugs regularly? If so, why?

We'd be remiss if we didn't scratch the surface on this topic and ask you to ask yourself these questions. Some medications are important and lifesaving, but many medications—complete with their laundry list of side-effects—are unnecessary and can be avoided with proper diet and exercise. Furthermore, if you're doing things that damage your body, then *you* will pay the price for it.

What You Do with Your Body

We all know sitting on the couch, eating potato chips, and watching TV isn't the path to a healthy lifestyle. But there is a common misconception that you must live on the other side of the exercise continuum to be healthy—as if you must run five miles every day, go to the gym seven days a week, and be able to bench press a small European vehicle to be fit. But this isn't true.

Defining Exercise

We aren't concerned with looking like body builders. Instead, we're concerned with being healthy, being fit, and feeling good about our physical fitness. Over the last few years, we've tried several things that have worked for us (and many other things that haven't), and during this time we determined the most important measurements of success were not measured in pounds on a scale, but rather by two things:

1. Are we constantly improving our fitness?
2. Are we happy with our progress?

That's how we measure our success. Because, face it, you could lose all the weight you want but still not be happy with your physical fitness. In fact, this happened to Joshua.

Through a combination of pescatarianism and intermittent fasting, Joshua lost 80 pounds over several years. On the surface this sounds great, and it certainly was a good thing. But, by 28, even though he was considerably lighter, he was flabby, doughy, and weak. But then, over two years, he developed small, simple, daily habits that transformed him into the best shape of his life by age 30.

Daily Exercise Habits

We've both tried a variety of exercise techniques to improve our health over the years. We've gone to the gym four to six times per week. We've attempted running, lifting weights, and playing sports. And the good news is they all work. Granted, some work better than others, but every exercise has been better than doing nothing at all (which was often what we did before—*nothing*).

After experimenting with different exercises for two years and speaking with several personal trainers, Joshua wrote about the daily exercise habits he had developed in an essay titled "18-Minute Minimalist Exercises." That essay outlined his simple exercise habits, including the three principles and four exercises he embraces daily.

Joshua's Exercise Principles

Enjoy exercise. I do only exercises I enjoy. I don't enjoy running, so I don't do it. I attempted it for six months and discovered it wasn't for me. If you see me running, call the police, because someone is chasing me. Instead, I find other ways to do cardio: I walk every day, I get on the elliptical machine at the gym, I do bodyweight exercises that incorporate cardio.

Exercise relieves stress. I use exercise as my primary means to kill stress. I love hitting the gym (or the park) in the evenings if I feel tense or stressed. Exercising at the end of a long, stressful day always gives me time in solitude to reflect on what's important.

Variety keeps exercise fresh. When I started exercising, I hit the gym three times per week, which was certainly better than not exercising at all. Then, as I got more serious, I went daily—about six times per week (even when I was working 70 hours a week). But this routine became too time consuming, and doing the same exercises over and over eventually caused me to plateau.

These days I mix it up: I walk quite a bit every day, and I still go to the gym a few times per week—but the variety of my daily eighteen-minute exercise has made the most noticeable difference.

Joshua's 18-Minute Exercises

Honestly, eighteen minutes sounds like an arbitrary number—because it is. When I started these bodyweight exercises, I didn't have a specific window of time in mind. But I timed myself and discovered that almost every time, I was worn out within eighteen minutes. Thus, these are my eighteen-minute exercises, all of which you can do in your living room, outdoors, or just about anywhere—even outside in the rain.

During my eighteen minutes, I usually alternate between the following exercises. You can, of course, pepper in your own favorites, as well. And, yes, these exercises are suitable for both men and women.

Push-ups. Two years ago I couldn't do a single push-up. Eventually I could do one (after a few weeks of modified push-ups). After a while, I made it to ten and then 20. Now I can do 50–100 consecutively. I tend to complete three to five sets each day, resulting in roughly 300 push-ups within my eighteen minutes.

Pull-ups. Two years ago I thought I'd never be able to do a pull-up. Eventually I learned how to do one by hanging from a pull-up bar, slowly building my strength. Soon I could do two and then four. I can do 12–20 in a row now, three to five sets each day, resulting in roughly 40–60 pull-ups within my eighteen minutes. I often use monkey bars at the park or a pull-up bar at home. I used to hate pull-ups; now it's my favorite exercise.

Squats. I recently started bodyweight squats, and I've already noticed a huge difference. I do only three or four sets of 20–30 right now, but I'll continue to work my way up, and I'll continue to grow.

I don't have a specific routine or plan, I just take a 30-second break between sets, bouncing from one exercise to the next. After about eighteen minutes I'm completely spent, and I feel great afterward. I get that incredible, tired feeling you get after a great workout. What used to be tedious is now exhilarating.

You can work your way up, even if you can't do a single pull-up or push-up. Everyone has eighteen minutes a day to focus on their health, right?

Sleep

People often forgo sleep to "accomplish" whatever it is they want to accomplish. But if it is your desire to live a healthy life—in the optimal condition to experience and enjoy life—then you will need adequate rest.

The amount of sleep your body requires varies by the individual. Some of the most compelling studies we've read indicate you should average eight to ten hours of sleep every night. The best essay we've seen about sleep is "How to Get Smarter, Sleep More, and Get More Sex," by Julien Smith, and it can be found online at inoveryourhead.net/sleep-is-awesome/.

The Musts of Health

We strongly believe in turning your *shoulds* into *musts*. When you want to change a habit—be it diet, exercise, or anything else —this change is the tipping point. It is the point at which you create enough leverage; the point at which something you put off becomes urgent, necessary, vital. This is the point at which change becomes a *must*.

On our website, we encourage people to create *must* lists for various areas of their lives (i.e., we encourage you to create a list of things on which you have procrastinated, and turn those *shoulds* into *musts*—find leverage so you can take action). There are very few *musts* with respect to your health, and these *musts* are fairly broad:

You must eat a nutritional diet to be healthy.
You must exercise regularly to be healthy.
You must eliminate harmful substances.
You must treat your body like it is your most precious possession—because it is.

We encourage you to create your own *must* list. What *must* you do to experience a better, healthier life?

CHAPTER 3: RELATIONSHIPS

The Importance of Relationships

Your relationships are the most important of the Five Values. Don't believe us? Let us prove it.

Imagine winning the lottery, getting into the best shape of your life, paying off your debts, moving into your dream home (on the beach, of course), and not needing to work another day in your life.

Now imagine you wake up tomorrow and you have nobody to share your new life with. No friends. No family. No loved ones. Oh, the heartache. You finally got "everything you ever wanted," but there's no one to share it with. Without your relationships, you are unable to live a meaningful life.

Defining Relationships

Sometimes people use the word *relationship* to connote a physical or intimate relationship, but, for the purposes of this book, we use a broader definition: your relationships are the people with whom you have frequent contact, the people around you—friends, partners, spouses, lovers, roommates, coworkers, acquaintances, or anyone you interact with on a regular basis.

We all want to be loved. We all want to love. And we all want to have other people with whom we share our experiences. Some of us (especially extroverts like Ryan) desire the love and attention of many relationships (his family, his close friends, his girlfriend, the people he mentors, etc.), while others (especially introverts like Joshua) desire the close connections of a select few relationships. Neither desire is right or wrong: your desire is based on your preferences, and no matter who you are, we all need personal relationships to thrive.

Reflecting on Past Relationships

The past does not equal the future. Living in the past is tantamount to driving using only the rearview mirror—eventually you will crash if you don't know what's going on in front of you.

Because of this, your past relationships aren't necessarily indicative of your future relationships. This is good news. Much of the time you don't think about why you're involved in a particular relationship—you just ended up there, and you accept that this is where you are, even when the relationship makes you unhappy.

You can learn from your past relationships, though. The good times tell you what went well and give you a strategy by which you can model your future. And the bad times help you identify how things went wrong and give you clues and social cues by which you can avoid bad relationships in the future. Everything is clearer in retrospect.

Three Ways to Create Better Relationships

There are three ways to create better relationships:

1. Find great new relationships.
2. Transform your current relationships.
3. Change who you are.

We will focus on all three possibilities throughout this chapter.

Evaluating Current Relationships

It's time to take an honest look at your current relationships. Do they make you happy? Do they satisfy you? Are they supportive? Do they help you grow? Do they contribute to your life in positive, meaningful ways? These are all important questions to consider while evaluating your current relationships.

Try this: make a three-column list of every relationship—big or small—in which you are involved:

Name. The first column will contain the person's name. Fill in this column first. Think of every person with whom you interact regularly. Your family, close friends, significant other, coworkers, bosses, teachers, that guy seven cubicles over who picks his nose when he thinks nobody's looking. Think about every aspect of your life. With whom do you interact? You might have 20 people in this column or you might have 400. Either way, spend some time and create your list.

Signifiers. Once the first column is complete, the second column will contain one of three signifiers for each person: *primary*, *secondary*, or *peripheral*.

The *primary* relationships, good or bad, are your closest relationships. This tier most likely includes your significant other, immediate and closest family members, and extremely close friends. Your *primary* relationships are the main characters in the movie of your life.

The *secondary* tier consists of relationships similar to the *primary* tier, except these relationships are of less value for a variety of reasons. Such relationships might include your close friends, your boss, a select few coworkers, and extended family members. Your *secondary* relationships are your supporting cast.

Chances are the vast majority of the people in your life will fall into the third category: the *periphery*. The *periphery* might include people like most coworkers, neighbors, members of your community, acquaintances, distant family members, and the like. These are the minor characters (and, occasionally, the extras) in your life's cast. You tend to respect their opinions and find at least some value in these relationships.

Effect. The third and final column on your list regards the effects of your relationships on your life. One of three effects goes in this column: *positive*, *negative*, or *neutral*.

Positive relationships make you happy and help you grow.

Negative relationships make you unhappy, unfulfilled, frustrated, or dissatisfied. They can stunt your personal growth.

Neutral relationships are somewhere between positive and negative. They don't necessarily make you unhappy, and most of the time you feel ambivalent toward the emotions you feel from them.

It's important to note that many close, *primary* relationships can be neutral or negative. That doesn't mean those relationships can't change, but just because someone is extremely close to you doesn't mean they foster a positive relationship—some of the most negative relationships reside in our top two tiers. Conversely, although many of your *peripheral* relationships will fall into the neutral category, other relationships in that tier might bring you great pleasure, resulting in a *positive peripheral* relationship.

What to Do with Your Current Relationships

Once your list is complete, review it and answer some important questions:

How many relationships do you have?
Why so many (or so few)?
What percentage are primary relationships?
What percentage are secondary relationships?
What percentage are peripheral relationships?
What percentage are positive relationships?
What percentage are negative relationships?
What percentage are neutral relationships?

Once you answer these questions, it's time to divide and conquer.

It's obvious your important relationships—negative or positive—are in your top two tiers, with the most important residing in the primary tier. But unfortunately, because the majority of your relationships reside in the periphery, you probably spend the majority of your time with your peripheral relationships. Consequently, if you're like most people, you focus most of your time, effort, and attention on the group of people who matters least to you.

This must change.

First, take a look at everyone in your peripheral tier. Are some of these folks people you'd like to see play a larger role in your life? Are they the people you'd like to have in your primary or secondary tiers? If so, what actions must you take to strengthen these relationships? What actions must you take to help them grow? Take a moment and consider these relationships.

Once you discover the peripheral relationships you want to move into your top two tiers, it's important to realize the role of the remaining people in your peripheral group. These are people you care about, people you wish great things for, but they are also people who consume the majority of your most precious commodity—your time. Thus, it is imperative you dedicate less time to this group and focus your attention on your primary and secondary tiers (including those people in the periphery who you want to move into those tiers). For some people, this might mean saying *no* more often, or turning down future commitments. For others, it might require a sit-down meeting explaining that you need your time back to focus on other aspects of your life. The idea here is to focus on creating the most meaningful relationships possible—relationships that will reside in your top two tiers.

Similarly, there are people in your primary and secondary tiers who likely don't belong there. It is up to you to decide which role these people play in your life. This is especially true for the relationships you labeled as *negative* relationships.

It is important to remember your relationships will not remain static for the rest of your life. People will shift in and out of your life, and shift within your relationship tiers as you grow and they grow. Many people who were especially relevant for you ten years ago are far less relevant today, right? Likewise, your future relationships will continue to shift, change, and grow. And so it's important that you play an active part in this process —that you're actively engaged in your relationship selection— which often includes making difficult decisions regarding the people in your top two tiers.

The Most Important Relationships

Your primary relationships are by far the most important relationships in your life. This is your core team—the people most important to you. The rest of this chapter will focus on these primary relationships (present and future). These are the people you love, the people for whom you would do anything. These relationships typically include:

Intimate relationships. Your lover, partner, spouse, significant other. This is typically the most important relationship in your life, and it should be treated accordingly.

Closest friends. We often call these people our best friend or best friends. This group of closest friends usually consists of fewer than five people with whom you are close and care about deeply. That platitude your parents recited—the one about being able to count your closest friends on one hand—is generally true.

Immediate family. Parents, children, and other close family members fall into this category.

A note about your *secondary* relationships: Your secondary relationships are important, as well (significantly more important than your *peripheral* relationships), but they should receive your time and attention only after your commitments to your *primary* relationships are fulfilled. Your primary relationships are your top priority. This might mean shifting one or two people from your *secondary* tier into your *primary* tier (or vice versa), if necessary.

Change Yourself, Not Others

You can't change the people around you, but you can change the people around you.

Sometimes you have to get rid of certain relationships, even relationships of great value. Sometimes a person's beliefs or values are radically different from yours. When this is the case it's okay to terminate the relationship, or at least to change the terms of the relationship.

We all change over time: sometimes we grow closer to certain people, sometimes we grow apart, sometimes we fall out of love, sometimes we evolve together. Just because someone has changed, doesn't mean they don't love you—it doesn't mean they don't care about you immensely—it simply means they've changed.

Moreover, you cannot expect a person to change in every way you want them to. Of course, some people make radical improvements in their lives, but it is not your responsibility in any relationship to expect someone to improve to adhere to your standards, beliefs, or values.

The only person you can change is yourself. When you lead by example, often the people closest to you will follow suit. If you improve your diet, start exercising, begin paying close attention to your important relationships, and set higher relationship standards, then you'll notice other people doing the same thing. If the best version of you shows up to the party, you'll bring the best out of other people.

Unfortunately, there will be times when certain relationships don't work—marriages, intimate relationships, close friendships, employee-boss relationships, relationships with family members, etc. The best thing you can do is change yourself (not attempt to "improve" the other person). You don't have to stay in a relationship if you are unhappy. That doesn't mean you shouldn't make an effort to get to the root of the relationship's problems; it means you can leave the relationship if it is not working.

Before you alter or terminate a relationship, you should envision what you'd like your relationships to look like in the future. The following sections discuss specific ideas for how to envision a new future for your relationships.

Relationship Growth

No matter how positive or negative your current relationships, you want them to improve so you have outstanding future relationships. Even the greatest relationships need to grow to remain great. In fact, the best relationships are always growing— that's one of the reasons they're so great. If your relationships aren't growing, they're dying. But when your relationships grow, you feel alive.

Seeking and Selecting Future Relationships

Without a vision, people perish. We've all heard that before. The same is true for our relationships, especially our *primary* relationships. Without a vision, you will settle for whatever is in front of you. Ergo, you need a distinct vision of what you want your relationships to be—what you want your relationships to look like. If your vision is compelling enough, you'll do anything to make it reality.

There are three things to consider when seeking new relationships (or improving current ones):

What do you want? At the surface, this seems like a trite question, but it is crucial. Write down everything you want from your primary relationships (intimate relationships, close friendships, and the like). What do they look like? What do you want to do together? What do you want from them mentally, physically, spiritually, emotionally? What types of desires must these people have? What are their beliefs, values, desires, interests, rules, fears?

What must *not* occur within the relationship? You can find everything you want in a person, but if they also carry a belief or value you must not have in your life, it can ruin the entire relationship. For example, say you find an intimate relationship and the other person appears to have everything you want, except they are unsupportive. If an unsupportive person is something you must not have, then that relationship will not work long-term. Now, make your list of things that must not occur in your relationships.

Who must you become to attract this kind of person? Once you've determined what you want and what you must not have, you must determine what changes you must make within yourself to attract this kind of person as a friend, lover, or whatever relationship you are searching for. Must you listen more? Must you get into better shape? Must you learn how to communicate better? Write down what you must change in your life to attract these new relationships.

Once you've answered these three questions, read this list daily. It's important to understand what you're seeking, what you want to avoid, and what you must change within yourself to get these results.

Making Passionate Relationships Work

Commonalities make relationships work, but differences make relationships exciting and passionate. You need both—commonalities and differences—to make passionate relationships work long-term.

Sometimes people enter into a relationship based solely on chemistry. Chemistry is associated with variety, and it's great initially; it's easy to be attracted to someone because they are different. Unfortunately, chemistry alone is not sustainable. Over time, too many differences can become annoying, frustrating, and troublesome. And, as we mentioned earlier, some differences in areas like values, beliefs, and individual needs can completely destroy a relationship in the long-run.

Conversely, sharing many commonalities with someone sounds great, but having too many things in common becomes boring. Being exactly alike lacks the requisite variety to keep your relationship passionate. Too often a relationship falls apart because, instead of working together as a team, the two people become extensions of each other, appendages that get in the way.

The best relationships share a healthy combination of commonalities and differences. While you embrace the things in common, you learn to respect and enjoy the differences. You will thus understand the balance of *certainty* and *variety* necessary for a sustainable, meaningful relationship.

Eight Elements of Great Relationships

Meaningful relationships have eight main elements that must be nurtured for the relationships to grow and improve: love, trust, honesty, caring, support, attention, authenticity, and understanding. The following eight sections discuss each of these elements.

Love

It is possible to dislike certain parts of a person and still love every piece of them. Your primary relationships require immense amounts of love. If you truly love someone, what are you willing to do for them? Anything! You should be willing to bend over backwards, to go to great lengths for the people you love. That's how you strengthen your relationships.

Furthermore, being *loved* is different from being *needed*. You should, however, work hard to understand what your loved ones need. And the primary relationships in your life should feel the same toward you. If they don't, you must ask yourself if that person is worthy of being one of your primary relationships, and worthy of the time you must dedicate to said relationships.

Trust

When you absolutely trust someone, you are open—you are the real you—which fosters the closest possible relationship. Trust breeds more trust, which encourages habitual honesty from both parties.

Honesty

To lie is to intentionally mislead someone when they expect honest communication. Sometimes it feels like it's easier to lie, but no matter the circumstance—no matter how small or big the lie is—lying is wrong and harmful to your relationships.

"Honesty is a gift we can give others. It is also a source of power and an engine of simplicity," Dr. Sam Harris wrote in his book, *Lying*. He continued by stating, "Knowing that we will attempt to tell the truth, whatever the circumstances, leaves us with little to prepare for. We can simply be ourselves."

Thus, not only is being honest the right thing to do in your relationships, it is also much simpler in the long run. And if a relationship isn't built on honesty, it isn't a relationship worth having.

Caring

This is the other side of trust. Caring is the most *active* element—the ultimate way to *contribute* to your relationship in a meaningful way. Caring means you are concerned enough about someone to express it through your consistent actions. Therefore, *caring* is a verb: your *actions* are how you show someone you care.

Call it compassion, call it sympathy, call it admiration—but whatever you call it, we all value someone who genuinely cares about us, about our feelings, about our lives. Ergo, we must *act* accordingly.

Support

The strongest relationships are mutually supportive relationships: meaning, not only do you care about the other person, but you are genuinely excited when they're excited, you're genuinely happy that they're happy, and you encourage them to grow as you grow, allowing you to grow side by side.

Attention

Much of the time, especially on our website, we talk about the importance of being present—the importance of living in the moment (see minimalists.com/be). Being present requires focus, concentration, attention.

This is especially true with your *primary* relationships. If these people are important enough to be in your top tier, then they are important enough to merit your undivided attention when you are engaged with them. No cellphone. No instant messaging. No texting. No watching the TV in your peripheral vision. Your relationships are important and they need to be treated accordingly. Hang on to their every word. You'll be pleasantly surprised with the reaction you get from people when you give them your full attention. (Additional reading, "Most Emergencies Aren't": minimalists.com/emergencies.)

Authenticity

Think of a person you respect for their honesty, their openness, their integrity. You know a few people like this, right? Pick one, and think about that person for a moment.

This person feels *real* to you. Genuine. Authentic. It's refreshing to be around this person, to get to know this person, to interact with them. We feel safe around authentic people, as if we could reveal to them our deepest, darkest secrets, as if we could trust them with anything.

And when we get to know these people on a deeper level—when we establish a connection with them—it's refreshing to discover they are who we thought they were, that beneath the surface they are authentically themselves.

Authentic people have no agenda, and yet they have aspirations. Authentic people are trustworthy, and yet sometimes they fall short. Authentic people are awesome, and yet sometimes they are superficial. Authentic people care enough to listen, and yet sometimes they don't hear everything. Authentic people can weather the storm, and yet they get wet.

Authentic people are passionate, content, carefree, calm, kind, and helpful—and yet authentic people are still people, they are human beings, and thus they worry, possess doubt, and make mistakes and bad decisions.

Authentic people are fallible. Authentic people are flawed. Authentic people are fearful. Authentic people are tempted by lust and greed—by all the trappings of this world.

None of us is perfect, but we all have the capacity to be authentic, to remove the pretense and the facade from our repertoire and just be authentically ourselves, not the people we think we're *supposed* to be.

Understanding

The final element is perhaps the most intricate and complicated because it is difficult to truly understand others. Hence, this section is meant to serve as a recipe for understanding others.

Arguments are a breeding ground for discontent. Yet many

arguments, especially with people we love, are birthed from simple misunderstandings blown out of proportion. To avoid this spiral of misunderstanding—and eventually arrive at a place of shared contentment—we must avoid acting on impulse, and we must instead work through the four stages of understanding:

Tolerate. Tolerance is a weak virtue, but it's a good start. If someone's behavior seems bothersome, it is best to avoid the knee-jerk reactions of fight or flight, and to instead find ways to tolerate their differences. For example, let's say you're an aspiring minimalist, but your partner is an enthusiastic collector—a clear dichotomy of beliefs. Your partner believes collecting porcelain figurines or vintage guitars is the bomb diggity; you believe their treasures are clutter. So you're left scratching your noggin, wondering how to convert them to your singularly valid viewpoint, which can be mind-numbingly frustrating. Don't worry, though, you needn't get on the same page right way; you need only understand you both have your reasons for being on separate pages. By tolerating someone's quirks, and allowing them to live happily within their own worldview, you may not *understand* their obsession with creepy statuettes or unplayed musical instruments, but at least you will be on a path toward understanding that person—and that's a big first step.

Accept. To truly live in concert with others, we must quickly move past tolerance toward acceptance. Once you've made a concerted effort to at least tolerate the other person's quirks, their beliefs begin to seem less silly and, in time, more meaningful—not meaningful to you, but meaningful to someone you care about. Once you realize your partner's collection has a purpose to them, it is easier to accept because it is a part of who they are as a whole person; and while you may not *like* a particular behavior, you still *love* the entire person, foibles and all.

Respect. Accepting—not just tolerating, but truly *accepting*—someone's idiosyncrasies is difficult, but not nearly as challenging as *respecting* that person *because* of their idiosyncrasies. Think about it: it took you this many years to arrive at your current credo, so it's unreasonable to expect someone else to meet you there overnight, no matter how cogent your counterargument. Okay, so perhaps you'd never hoard figurines or guitars, but there are many beliefs you hold that, at face value, seem ridiculous to someone else. But even when other people don't agree with you, even when they don't understand your stance, you still want them to respect your beliefs, right? So why not extend that same respect to the people you love? Only then will you move closer to understanding; only then will you begin to realize your worldview isn't the solitary axiom by which everyone must live. Sure, it's nice to have a clutterfree home, but it's even nicer to share your life with people you respect.

Appreciate. With respect in your rearview, understanding is right around the bend. Continuing our example, let's say your partner experiences great joy from their collection. Why would you want to change that? You want them to be happy, right? Well, if their collection brings contentment to their life, and if you truly care about that person, then their collection should bring joy to your life, too, because happiness is contagious—but only after you get past the arguments, past the stages of tolerance, acceptance, and respect, and you honestly appreciate the other person's desires, values, and beliefs. Many of us navigate different roads toward happiness, but even if we travel separate routes, it is important we appreciate the journey—not only ours, but the journey of everyone we love. When we appreciate others for who they are, not who we want them to be, then, and only then, will we *understand.*

So the next time you reach a fork in the road, remember T.A.R.A.: Tolerate, Accept, Respect, and Appreciate. If you travel this path frequently, your relationships will flourish, and you'll experience a richness of experience that wasn't possible without a deep understanding of the people in your life.

This path works not only for significant others, but for friends, coworkers, and anyone else with whom we want to strengthen our connection. Of course there will be times when values clash, and you won't be able to appreciate the person for who they are. And there will even be rare times when T.A.R.A. is the wrong path altogether: if someone engages in self-destructive behavior—drugs, crime, racism—then you should *not* appreciate their conduct. Sometimes it's okay to say goodbye, walk away, and travel a perpendicular path.

Ultimately, *understanding* answers the important questions about relationships: *What drives the other person? What do they want? What do they need? What excites them? What are their desires? What are their pains? What do they enjoy? What makes them happy?* If you can answer these questions, you'll be better equipped with the understanding you need to meet their needs. If you meet someone's needs, and they meet yours, you're guaranteed to have a vibrant, passionate, growing relationship.

Nourish Your Relationships

It is important to keep in mind that you must find ways to continuously nourish your primary relationships every day. They are far too important to ignore. If you focus on the above eight elements, you will strengthen your relationships more than you thought possible. Sure, it takes a considerable amount of hard work, focus, and time, but having meaningful relationships is worth every bit of effort you put into them.

Additional Reading: Relationships

- Goodbye Fake Friends: minimalists.com/fake
- Letting Go of Relationships: minimalists.com/relationships
- Prepared to Walk Away: minimalists.com/walk-away

CHAPTER 4: PASSIONS

The Importance of Cultivating Your Passions

Cultivating your passions is the most important of the Five Values. Don't believe us? Let us prove it.

Imagine winning the lottery, getting into the best shape of your life, finding your soulmate, establishing the most meaningful relationships possible, paying off your debts, moving into your dream home (on the beach, of course), and not needing to work another day in your life.

Now imagine you wake up tomorrow and the next day and then the next day with nothing to do, nothing to be excited about, nothing to fuel your fire. Oh, the horror. There are only so many TV shows you can watch or vacations you can take before you realize passion is missing from your life, before you realize your life lacks meaning. You will not feel fulfilled if your life lacks passion. This is often the root cause of that empty feeling so many people experience.

What You Call Your Work

Back to reality. Let's take a look at your average day. How do you spend it? Do you work the typical nine-to-five? Do you stay at home with the kids? Do you run your own business?

Whatever you do, the level of passion you have for what you do can sometimes be measured by the label you give your work. People tend to designate one of three labels to their work: *job*, *career*, or *mission*. When you speak about your work, which term do you use? Do you have a job? Do you have a career? Or are you one of the few who calls their work their mission?

Chances are you have a job—the daily grind. Or, if you're unemployed, you're probably looking for a job. It's a cultural imperative, the mythical American Dream—it's what we're "supposed" to do. We're taught to work extraordinarily hard in high school and then college, doing stuff we don't care about, so we'll find a "good job," one with reliable pay, solid benefits, and maybe even a retirement plan. And then we're supposed to work that soul-crushing job for 40 years so one day we might be able to retire and enjoy our lives for a few years (insurance actuarial studies have shown the average life span of a retiree is often only three years after retirement). We're taught to work back-breakingly hard for a nonliving entity, donating our most precious commodity (our time) for a paycheck. We're taught that there is much more value in that paycheck—and all the *stuff* that paycheck can buy us—than there is in actuality.

The truth is we all need money to live: there's no doubt we all need to pay for a roof over our heads, food to nourish our bodies, clothes to keep us warm, medical care when we're sick or injured, and various other essentials. But the aforementioned cycle—what we've been sold as the "American Dream"—is devoid of meaning. The American Dream will not make you happy. In fact, for many, the pursuit of this set of ideals is oppressive and is guaranteed to be a losing enterprise.

The Ugly Roots of a Career

If what you do everyday is just a *job*, then it is difficult to feel fulfilled during your working hours. Even if you work really, really hard and establish a *career* for yourself, you'll likely have a hard time creating a meaningful life within the confines of your work schedule. In fact, having a career is one of the most dangerous things you can do if you want to find meaning in your life.

Careers are dangerous because people invest so much of themselves into their careers that they establish an identity and a social status based upon their job title.

Think about it: one of the first things a person asks when you're becoming acquainted is *What do you do?* On the surface, this seems like an innocent enough question, doesn't it? But the implied question isn't *What do you do?* which by itself is rather expansive and could encompass thousands of things (I volunteer at soup kitchens, I work at Walmart, I enjoy fishing on the weekends, I exercise five days a week, I drink water, etc.); the implied question is *What do you do for a living?* or *Where do you work?* which is vastly different from the question itself. This "innocent" question actually says, *I will judge you as a person by how you make your money, and I will assign a particular social status to you based on your occupation.*

People are asked to answer this question so often that they become rooted in their careers: they establish "what they do" as their core identity, and they give their occupations far more societal worth than they deserve. Once someone establishes their career as who they are as a person, it is difficult to shed that identity, even if the person hates their career (*I don't want to work here, but this is just who I am!*).

Thankfully, there are better ways to answer the *What do you do?* question. We have found people are programmed to ask this question without giving it any thought; it's not much different from asking *How are you doing?* So the best thing to do is to get the other person to actually think about the mindless question they just posited. When presented with this question, the two of us tend to answer with another question, such as, "That's a rather expansive question. What do you mean by it?" or "That's an expansive question; perhaps we could discuss it over a cup of coffee." Another way to answer this question is by stating what you're passionate about, instead of spouting off what your vocation is. So, instead of saying, "I'm a Director of Operations," say, "I'm passionate about writing (or scrap-booking or rock climbing or whatever you're passionate about)." It's nice to follow that statement with, "What are you passionate about?" This response completely redirects the conversation, changing its trajectory from *what you both do* to *what you're both passionate about*, which is far more interesting.

Such responses immediately cause the person to reconsider the question, while simultaneously helping you remember you are far more than your career. You are a mother, a father, a sister, a brother, a spouse, a lover, a healthy person, a growing person, a contributing person, a passionate person with a meaningful life. You are not your career.

By changing your own thought process around this question, you can dig out those noxious roots that every career has. Over time you can remove your identity from your career and put it into its appropriate place—your life. Your identity should come from your meaningful life, not from how you earn a paycheck. (Additional thoughts on this topic: minimalists.com/do.)

Joshua & Ryan's Passions

Whether you follow our website or were just introduced to our writing with this book, you know our story by now. You know we worked corporate careers with fancy titles and sizable paychecks. But therein lies a clue: we had *careers*. What level of passion do you think we had spending our days focused on our careers instead of living our mission?

Sure, we worked hard, slaving 70 or more hours a week for a corporation. Sure, we enjoyed certain aspects of our careers. And sure, we often felt fortunate to have such "nice" careers at a young age, even though we didn't have college degrees. But, ultimately, we weren't satisfied by what we did for a living. We weren't living our mission.

We didn't feel fulfilled by our careers, so we turned to society's idea of living: we bought stuff, spent too much money, and lived paycheck to paycheck trying to purchase happiness in every trip to the shopping mall or luxurious vacation we could find. Instead of cultivating a passion, instead of searching for our mission, we pacified ourselves with ephemeral indulgences, inducing an excitement that didn't last far past the checkout line.

Eventually we discovered our passion—and thus our mission —was waiting far beyond the sea of consumption, but first we had to remove a lot of anchors before we could navigate our way to clearer waters.

Joshua has a passion for writing. Ryan has a passion for mentoring others. Once we discovered our passions, we were able to shape them into our mission over a two-year period.

The Confluence of Passion and Mission

It's important to note we don't subscribe to the notion that working for a corporation is bad or evil.

We also don't believe you were "meant" to be passionate about one particular thing, or that you have one "true calling" in life.

Rather, we believe you can be passionate about virtually anything. Consequently, any line of work can be your mission. Just because something sounds boring to one person doesn't mean it's not exciting and rewarding for another. It is perfectly plausible to think that someone can be deeply passionate about accounting the same way another person might be passionate about horseback riding. Neither sound very exciting to us, but that doesn't mean there aren't people who are passionate about both.

Occasionally, people stumble into a line of work that brings them ultimate satisfaction. These people who are paid to do what they love tend to refer to their work as their mission. Is that you? If so, congratulations—you are one of the few. If you don't, however, feel grateful and passionate about the day's work, then chances are you have not found (or are not cultivating) your mission.

The rest of this chapter is dedicated to helping you find and then cultivate your passions, and to pursue your mission.

This journey is easy for some people. These people already know what they're passionate about, but perhaps aren't yet pursuing that passion as their full-time mission.

Conversely, this journey is sometimes the hardest part for other people. Some people don't know what they want to do, they don't know what they're passionate about, they have no clue what their mission is.

No matter where you fall on this continuum, the rest of this chapter will help you identify the anchors holding you back from discovering and cultivating your passions.

A Misconception About Passionate People

A common misconception is that people who are passionate about what they do are inherently that way. That misconception is illogical: it couldn't be further from the truth.

People who are passionate about what they do are, in most ways, just like people who aren't passionate about their work. Some days passionate people don't want to get out of bed; sometimes they don't feel like starting work on the new project that's looming in front of them. Other days they jump out of bed feeling excited and motivated by their mission.

In other words, passionate people are just like you.

Passion Fuels More Passion

There are, however, two distinct differences that distinguish passionate people from uninspired people.

First, passionate people know what they are passionate about. Boiled down to that last sentence, this statement might sound obvious, but, truth be told, no one is passionate about only *one* thing. Joshua isn't passionate only about writing; he's passionate about many creative pursuits. Similarly, Ryan's sole passion doesn't lie with mentoring people; he's passionate about snowboarding and wakeboarding and longboarding and pretty much anything with a board (except waterboarding). Passionate people know what they are *most* passionate about, but they also know what else they are passionate about: they know what gets them excited, what gets them energized, what gets them into a peak state.

Second, passion fuels more passion. Passionate people turn to their passions when they are feeling uninspired. On those days when they don't want to get out of bed or start that new project, passionate people focus on the things that get them excited. For example, there were times during the creation of this book—particularly while editing the first few drafts—that seemed especially monotonous. Instead of waiting to be inspired by a sudden burst of passionate activity, we chose to continue our trek through the murky waters of monotony, all the while keeping an eye on what we knew we were passionate about. In fact, it was our passions that acted as a beacon—by dredging through the tedium, we were able to stay focused on what was important. Without our passions guiding us, it would have been easy to veer off course and never return. By the end of the final draft of this book, we were both excited about our creation and what it would mean to the people we shared it with.

Using what you're passionate about to keep you focused and fuel more passion is a critical part in discovering your mission. But first you must discover what you're passionate about.

Removing Anchors to Find Your Passion

It is often difficult to discover your passions because we tend to get stuck in the laboriousness of our daily routines. It's easy to embrace the uninspiring, lifeless cycle of your everyday work—

day in, day out. It's easy to get anchored by our daily lives, and it's much harder to free ourselves of those anchors.

As it turns out, we discovered four main anchors in our own lives that were keeping us from pursuing our passions: identity, status, certainty, and money.

Removing the Anchor of Identity

Who are you? Have you ever thought about this question? On the surface it sounds fairly simple, but in reality it's a salient question—and it's not an easy one to answer. Because of the complexity of this question, we often turn to our vocation for an answer: I'm a teacher, I'm an accountant, I'm a stay-at-home mom. While these are acceptable answers to a different question (i.e., *What do you do to earn a paycheck?* or *How do you spend the majority of your time?*), they become problematic when we give these labels enough meaning to say *That's who I am as a person.*

Once you acknowledge your vocation is who you are, it's extraordinarily difficult to do something else. This is one of the reasons people stay in the same industry when they change jobs (I wasn't happy as a sales manger at ABC Paper Company, but I bet I'll be happy as a sales manager at XYZ Paper Company!). People get so wrapped up in their vocation as their identity that it's hard for them to realize they are so much more—they are beautiful in so many ways.

When you're trapped in this kind of identity, it's hard to realize you are not your job, you are not your stuff, you are not your debt, you are not your paycheck—you are so much more. You are a brother, a father, a mother, a sister, a lover, a partner, a friend, a creator, a contributor, a human being capable of so much more.

For the two of us, this meant actively identifying ourselves with more meaningful labels than our corporate-given titles like *director* or *manager*. This meant we had to publicly identify ourselves with meaningful labels such as *mentor*, *leader*, *contributor*, and *minimalist*.

What other meaningful labels can you use to identify yourself? Once you shed the tyranny of identity, you will clear a path to remove your other anchors.

Removing the Anchor of Status

As people climb their corporate ladders, as they get more tenure and familiarity and comfort in their jobs and careers, they tend to experience a strange phenomenon: they associate status with their vocation above anything else. They feel their career makes them important and significant. This is why so many people feel ashamed, embarrassed, insignificant, and even depressed when they lose their job. Sure, they worry about money and how they're going to make a living, but after the initial panic over money subsides, they feel empty and insignificant without their job. That's because people often give significance to something that is relatively unimportant.

If you're caught in the clutches of status, it's hard to see there are other aspects of your life that are far more important than your profession (e.g., the Five Values covered in this book —health, relationships, passions, growth, and contribution—are all markedly more important). People frequently associate an appreciable amount of social status to their employment because it's the easiest thing to control in the moment. That is, if you work hard (even if it's for a job you hate), then you're rewarded with instant gratifications (awards, rewards, praise from the boss, public recognition, private recognition, coworker envy, coworker sucking-up, perceived power, additional responsibilities, and the like), as well as long-term gratifications (raises, bonuses, commissions, promotions, incentives, fringe benefits, etc.).

Unfortunately, many of the most important things in life are (a) much more difficult to control than short-term hard work at your job, and (b) don't provide the same instant gratification as the status of a career. Societally, you've been programmed to want (or even expect) immediate results. Furthermore, these same social imperatives place far more emphasis on career and monetary status than status of any other sort.

Take, for example, a stay-at-home dad. What's the first thing that comes to your mind? Chances are it's something like, *That sure must be nice!* or *He sure is lucky!* or *He isn't behaving like a real man!* or *He is lazy!* But anyone who knows a competent stay-at-home dad knows these judgments are far from the truth. Conversely, when you think of a CEO you probably think *He is rich!* or *He has a lot of power!* or *He worked very hard to get there!* While none of these things are necessarily true, either, it's a cultural stereotype that's hard to escape.

The best way to escape the destructive influence of status, and the cultural stereotypes that come along with it, is to turn down the volume. For the two of us, this meant placing less value on what people thought about our jobs, and showing them why they should give more credence to our new identities, which were transferable to virtually anything we did, not just our careers.

Once you embrace this more positive notion of status, you will more easily be able to embrace more variety in your life; you will be able to embrace a higher level of uncertainty, and you will be able to sacrifice some of the certainty that is anchoring you down.

Removing the Anchor of Certainty

Certainty is a strange thing. Everyone needs some level of certainty to survive. You must be certain your ceiling isn't going to collapse while you're sleeping, you must be certain your drinking water isn't poisonous, you must be certain the car approaching you won't veer over the yellow line into your lane.

But beyond our basic needs for safety, the level of certainty people need varies drastically person by person. Most people require vast amounts of certainty—far too much certainty—to feel safe, while other people (like, for example, professional skydivers and race car drivers) require very little certainty in their daily lives. The latter group will be able to remove the anchor of uncertainly fairly easily, but the former group will need to step outside their comfort zone to remove this debilitating anchor from their lives.

Certainty feels nice—it makes you feel comfortable, it makes you feel warm and fuzzy—but it's sometimes the biggest underlying reason you don't make the changes you want to make. That is, you're not happy with your current situation, but you're comfortable enough that you don't want to sacrifice your comfort today for something that could potentially be less comfortable tomorrow, and thus you don't change.

In other words, you associate more pain with changing than you associate pleasure with the change. Fortunately, there are two ways to alter this thought process—two ways to cut loose from the anchor of certainty so you can change your life.

First, you can find a way to associate more pain with *not*

changing. You can do so by looking at the potential loss of meaning in your life—the loss of not accomplishing what you truly want to accomplish, the loss of not pursuing your passion, the loss of not living your mission. The reality is that the long-term pain of regret far outweighs the short-term pleasure of certainty.

Second, you can associate more pleasure with the long-term fulfillment of pursuing your passions and living your mission.

Either option—or a combo of the two—will give you the leverage you need.

For us, this meant two different things: Joshua leaped without having much of a plan. He decided the pain of not pursuing his passions was no longer worth the certainty his corporate career provided. Conversely, Ryan slowly eased out of his corporate restraints, slowly associating more and more pleasure with the pursuit of his passions. (Read more about our exiting the corporate world at minimalists.com/quit.)

Removing the Anchor of Money

When you boil it down, money is simply another layer of certainty. But it's worth identifying as its own anchor—because of the stronghold it places on so many people, because of the importance our culture places on money, because it's typically the number one reason for someone to continue doing something they hate. *I gotta pay the bills!* is a lame excuse. Of course you need to make a living, but you will be able to do so while pursuing your passion.

The best way to remove the anchor of money is to give money less importance in your life. We were able to accomplish this by developing a detailed, five-step plan to regain control of our finances.

Money: it tears families apart, ruins marriages, and keeps people from pursuing their dreams. Money troubles inject unnecessary stress, anxiety, and arguments into our daily lives, which keeps us in perpetual discontent. We never seem to have enough, and, living paycheck to paycheck, we can't ever get ahead.

But it doesn't have to be this way.

We know this first hand. The road to financial freedom was a long trek for each of us. Even though we had prestigious six-figure careers, we struggled with money back then; we weren't financially free for a long time. It wasn't until we walked away from those careers (after devising a plan, of course) that we discovered how to get out of debt, how to eliminate unnecessary expenses, how to plan for our future, how to master our finances.

While we all need to make money to live—and there's certainly nothing wrong with earning a great salary—taking control of your financial life involves much more than adjusting your income upward: it involves making consistently good decisions with the resources you have, changing your financial habits, and living deliberately. None of which is inherently *easy* —especially under the tyranny of today's instant-gratification culture—but fortunately, regaining control of your finances is *simple*.

A few years ago, overwhelmed by money's rapacious tug on our lives, the two of us decided to change: we decided to take back control of our finances and our lives. These are the five steps we took, and they are the same principles we use today to ensure we'll never again struggle with money.

Step 1. BUDGET. Most of us have no idea where our money is going: we think we know, but we don't really know. This is doubly true for those of us who are married or are living with a significant other. So, the first step toward financial freedom is establishing a written monthly budget. Note the three key words here: written, monthly, and budget.

A few guidelines:

Categories. Identify what's truly necessary by identifying all of your monthly expenses based on the past six months, and then divide your expenses into three categories, as outlined in our essay, "Need, Want, Like" (minimalists.com/want). Write down every expense (food, housing, utilities, insurance, cars, gas, transportation, clothes, credit cards, phones, Internet, pets, entertainment, etc.); triple-check the list with your significant other or a friend; and then use your Need, Want, Like categories to prioritize and cut where you can. The stricter you are, the sooner you'll be free.

Boundaries. Give every dollar a destination at the beginning of the month. By establishing these boundaries, you won't worry about what you can and can't purchase because money that wasn't assigned at the beginning of the month can't be spent mid-month.

Teamwork. Everyone in your household—even your children— must have a say in the written budget. This is the only way to get every person's buy-in. Working together means taking from one category to fund another (e.g., extracting money from, say, your clothing budget to fund your entertainment budget) until each person is on the same page. Once everyone is on board—once everyone is committed to financial freedom—it is much easier to gain the traction you need.

Adjust. You'll have some slip-ups along the way—that's all right, it's part of the process. At first, you and your family should scrutinize your written budget daily—and, eventually, weekly—adjusting accordingly until your whole family is comfortable with your set monthly allocations. The first month is the most difficult, but by the third month you'll curse yourself for wasting so much money during your budget-less days.

Safety. It's best to create a Safety Net savings account with $500–$1000 for emergencies. Do *not* touch this money unless there is a true emergency (car repairs, medical bills, job loss, etc.). Your Safety Net will allow you to stay on budget even when life punches you in the face. Over time, once you're out of debt (step three below), your Safety Net will grow to include several months of income. But for now, worry only about the first $500–$1000 to start, which you'll want to keep in a separate Safety Net account to avoid temptation.

Step 2. PAY YOURSELF (INVEST). Most of us hear the word *invest* and we panic. Investing seems so complicated, so abstract, so not-something-I-can-wrap-my-head-around. Instead of thinking of it as *investing money*, think of it as *paying your future self*. And with today's online tools, you needn't be overwhelmed —investing is easier than ever. Anyone can (and must) do it.

We both use a simple online-investment tool as our personal savings, planning, and investing software. We invest our money into four separate buckets using online software: Safety Net, Retirement Fund, House Fund, and Wealth-Building Fund (visit minimalists.com/retirement to learn more about our specific investment strategy, as well as some free tools we use to keep us on track).

Right now is the best time to start planning for your future. Whether you're planning for retirement, starting a business, saving for a home, building a larger Safety Net, or focusing on long-term wealth-building, now is the best time to begin. Not next week, not tomorrow—today. Even if you have no money to invest, you must devise a plan to begin investing in your future self. The best way to do this is to automate your investments, which takes the guesswork out of investing. The future won't wait: do it today. Even if that means 1% of your income, or just $20 a month, to start. Your future self will thank you.

Step 3. DEBT-FREE. Contrary to what some academics might tell you, there is no such thing as "good debt." Let's say that again (read it out loud): THERE IS NO SUCH THING AS GOOD DEBT. Some debt is worse than other debt, but it's never "good."

You will not feel free until you are debt-free. The debtor is always slave to the lender. Besides, it feels amazing to have no car payments, no credit-card payments, and no student-loan payments looming in the shadows of your lifestyle.

Throughout our twenties we both had excessive piles of debt —more than six figures each. It was a debilitating feeling—a complete loss of freedom.

Although there are no magic bullets, the strategy we've seen work best is Dave Ramsey's book, *Total Money Makeover*, a detailed, step-by-step formula that both of us used to create a detailed plan, cut up our credit cards, and face our debts head-on. (You can also read Joshua's debt-free story at minimalists.com/debt.)

Step 4. MINIMIZE. Of course minimalism was a key component in our own journeys toward financial freedom. By clearing the clutter from our lives, we were able to focus on eliminating debt, changing our habits, and making better decisions with fewer resources.

We also learned that by simplifying—by identifying which material possessions weren't adding value to our lives—we were able to more quickly become debt-free by selling more than half our stuff locally (yard sales, consignment shops, flea markets) and online (eBay, Craigslist, Autotrader).

No, minimalism is not about deprivation—we don't want anyone to "live without" in the name of minimalism—but sometimes it makes sense to temporarily deprive ourselves of temporary satisfactions when we are attempting to move our lives in a better direction.

For example, as we were tackling our debts, Joshua sold his oversized house and moved into a tiny apartment. Ryan sold his fancy new car and purchased a decade-old vehicle without a monthly payment. We both jettisoned our cable subscriptions, satellite radio, and other luxury bills, which saved us hundreds of dollars each month. We also did "strange" things like deliver pizzas, work overtime, and find other ways to supplement our income in the short-term so we could pay off our debts faster. Plus, we sold hundreds of items—electronics, furniture, clothes, DVDs, books, collectibles, tools, yard equipment—that weren't essential, and we used that money to further pay down our debts. Anything that wasn't nailed to the floor found its way to eBay. Now everything we own serves a purpose or brings us joy, and we don't miss any of the trinkets of yesteryear.

Don't know how to start minimizing? Visit our "Start Here" page at minimalists.com/start for tips and best practices.

Step 5. CONTRIBUTE. The shortest path toward freedom is appreciating what you already have. One of the best ways to find gratitude for the gifts you've already been given is to change your perspective.

To do so, donate your most precious asset: your time. Bring your family to a local soup kitchen, food bank, or homeless shelter. Tutor less-privileged children in your city. Help the elderly with groceries or in-home care. Work on low-income houses with Habitat for Humanity. There are more resources than ever to help you contribute beyond yourself—just do an Internet search for volunteer opportunities in your area.

Whatever you do to build your contribution muscle, it needn't be grandiose—it need only contribute to someone else's life. If you do this for a few weeks, you'll realize your financial problems are tiny compared to many of the problems in the world around you. By discovering the smallness of your financial woes, you'll feel empowered to take massive action and beat the crap out of your relatively minor problems.

In a short period of time—two or three years—your entire life can radically transform from what it is today. All it takes is a plan (which you now have), determination (i.e., turning your *shoulds* into *musts*), and consistent action in the right direction.

Financial freedom isn't easy, but you knew that before reading this book. The exciting part about these five steps is they apply to anyone, anywhere on the socioeconomic ladder. Whether you earn minimum wage or six figures, whether you are single or have half-a-dozen children, we have seen these principles work for thousands of people—because it's not about our income level, it's about the decisions we make with the resources we have.

You are now equipped with a recipe to make outstanding financial changes, which will help you remove the anchor of money. You are obviously welcome to add your own ingredients to taste, but when it comes to true financial freedom, these five ingredients—budget, invest, eliminate debt, minimize, contribute—are nonnegotiable. All five are necessary.

Yes, you still have a considerable amount of research and planning and hard work ahead of you—but, most important, you must take action today. Diligence is paramount.

Finding Your Passion

Once you've removed your anchors, the horizon becomes vividly clear, which allows you to focus on finding your passion.

The first question we typically ask people is a fairly standard question: What would you do with your life if money wasn't an object? Most people who are searching for their passions are still deeply anchored to some (if not all) of the four anchors mentioned above, which causes them to articulate a fairly common response: I don't know.

If you don't know, it's likely because you're still anchored. Perhaps you're afraid of what people will say if you tell them you want to be a rodeo clown (for years Joshua never told people he wanted to be a writer, for fear of what they might think). Perhaps you're uncertain about the stability you'll have as a mascot for a professional baseball team. Perhaps you're worried you won't make enough money to feel significant. Whatever your anchors are, you must get rid of them to find your passion.

Once you've shed your anchors, you'll be able to answer the above question. Sometimes it's easier to answer that question if it's asked in a different way. Write down your answers to the following:

When was the last time you felt true excitement?
What were five other (different) experiences like this?
Why were you excited each of those times?
Which experiences excited you for the longest duration?
Was there a common thread among these excitements?
What did excitement look like? (How did your physiology change in these situations? How was your posture? Your facial expressions? Your breathing? Your heart rate? What else was happening with your body?)

Once you know what excitement looks and *feels* like, and you're able to relate it to specific experiences that have excited you, it's easier to answer the question *What would you do with your life if money wasn't an object?* Answer: *I'd do things that excited me every day.* So, what excites you the most for the longest period of time? That is likely your passion.

Said another way, passion is one half love, one half obsession. So what would you love to do each day? What would you be obsessed by? Where those intersect, that is your passion.

Now slap on that rodeo clown outfit and let's figure out how to turn it into your mission.

Turning Your Passion into Your Mission

We know what you're thinking: *That's great, but no one is going to pay me to be a rodeo clown/hula dancer/(insert real passion here).* Oh, really? Maybe not with that attitude. The truth is someone is earning a living doing the thing you're passionate about—doing the thing you obsessively love.

But they just got lucky! Well, maybe some of them got lucky, and maybe some were at the right place at the right time, but even luck has a recipe for continued success. Plus, there are thousands of people pursuing your passion (and making a good living from it) who didn't get lucky, who didn't achieve stardom or get everything they wanted overnight. They put in a ton of work, experienced debilitating failures and losses, and obsessively followed that beacon of passion until they were able to call it their full-time mission. Why not learn from those people?

If you want to learn how to turn your passion into your mission, the fastest, most efficient way is to emulate someone already doing it. It's called *modeling*, and that's what we did. We saw the likes of Colin Wright, Leo Babauta, Tammy Strobel, and Joshua Becker doing what we wanted to do— writing and contributing to people in meaningful ways—and we knew they already had a recipe for success; we knew they had learned through trial and error, and thus we knew we could learn from their successes and failures. Over the course of a year we met with each of these people face to face—all of whom lived thousands of miles away—and learned from their experiences. We bought them coffee or lunch and offered to add value in any way we could. We took copious notes and thanked them for adding value to our lives. We stayed in contact with these folks via email, phone, Skype, social media, etc., establishing a stronger bond over time. After meeting them and learning from their experiences, it became clear to us what we needed to do to turn our passions into our mission. That's when we took action; that's when we created our website and worked to add value to other people's lives through our writing and other content.

Your assignment is to do the same: find at least three people making a living doing what you're passionate about. It doesn't have to be anything similar to what we did. Your passion doesn't need to include a website or writing or online commerce. The specific nature of your passion is irrelevant. What's important is that you find people doing what you want to do, that you learn from them, that you soak up their knowledge, and that you take massive action.

It Ain't That Easy

You might be thinking: *But, guys, this is easier said than done!*

Yes, it's easier said than done: we know because we've done these things ourselves. We went from being anchored by debt and status and careers we weren't passionate about to pursuing our passions and living our mission. We now make less money, and we sometimes put more hours into the work week than we did at our original corporate jobs, but we love what we do and we obsess over it, so it certainly doesn't feel like a job.

Of course it wasn't easy—it took action to remove those anchors; it took courage to reject certain social imperatives so we could live meaningful lives. But it was worth it, and it's worth it for you, too. You deserve to pursue your passions, you deserve to live your mission, you deserve to live a meaningful life.

Additional Reading: Cultivating Passion

- 'Follow Passion' Is Crappy Advice: minimalists.com/cal
- 20 Questions for a Minimalist: minimalists.com/20q
- An Extraordinary Life: minimalists.com/extraordinary

CHAPTER 5: GROWTH

The Meaning of Life

We saved the most important two chapters for last: Growth and Contribution. These two values work hand-in-hand to form the meaning of our lives: to grow as individuals, and to contribute to others.

The Importance of Personal Growth

Growth is the most important of the Five Values. Don't believe us? Let us prove it.

Imagine winning the lottery, getting into the best shape of your life, finding your soulmate, establishing the most meaningful relationships possible, paying off your debts, moving into your dream home (on the beach, of course), finding the thing that makes you the most passionate, and discovering your mission in life.

Now what? Sit back and fish at the lake every day? Eat Cheetos and bask in the bluish glow of your television? Of course not. You want to continue to enjoy your newfound life— the one with the improved health, improved relationships, and newly discovered passions. Thus, you must continue to improve; you must continue to grow. If you're not growing, you're dying; and if you're dying, then, by definition, you're not living a meaningful life.

Incremental Changes

Once you make a change in your life, the journey isn't over—you must continue making changes if you want to be happy long-term. Think about all the changes you've already made, many of which might have seemed impossible five or ten years ago. How were you able to make those changes? Chances are you made the change one of two ways: giant leaps or baby steps.

Giant Leaps

There are some changes you can make that are huge and immediate. Take, for example, ending a relationship, quitting your job on the spot, picking up and moving to a new city, making a large purchase (a home or a car), and the like. We won't focus on these types of giant leap changes in this chapter. While sometimes these changes are necessary, there is generally only one way the *giant leaps* approach is successful: wait until the time is right and leap. Thus, we will focus on the most important changes in your life: the baby steps—because it's the baby steps that allow you to eventually take the giant leaps.

Daily Incremental Changes

Most change happens gradually, wherein you don't take a one-time giant leap, but you make small, gradual changes in your everyday life which amount to massive changes over time.

For example, no one goes to the gym, exercises really hard for one session, and expects to be fit for the rest of their life. It doesn't work that way. Similarly, most changes you make are about improving upon past changes in small ways every day.

The vast majority of the changes we've made in our lives—from our health to our jobs and our relationships—have involved these daily incremental changes. As you make these changes, your day-by-day life doesn't change considerably, but when you glance at your life in the rearview, everything is different.

Finding Leverage

The first step in any change, big or small, is making the *decision* to change. We're talking about making a real decision—one in which you make the change a *must* in your life—not something you *should* change *someday* when it becomes convenient for you.

Making these decisions can be easy or difficult, depending on one major factor: leverage.

Leverage is your ability to associate enough satisfaction with the change that you have no choice but to make the change a *must* in your life (e.g., "I *must* exercise" is appreciably different from "I *should* exercise"). The more leverage you have, the easier the decision is to make and follow through with—because the satisfaction you'll experience on the other side of the change is so great that you *must* make the change a reality.

When a change doesn't last, it's because the person doesn't see enough long-term benefit from the change (i.e., they don't associate enough satisfaction with the change, or they associate too much dissatisfaction with making the change).

But once you associate an immense amount of satisfaction with a change, it becomes a *must* for you. For example, the satisfaction of living a healthy lifestyle was enough for us to make considerable dietary and exercise changes in our lives. To get this leverage, we associated dissatisfaction with our current states (i.e., the way we looked in the mirror, the way we felt after a big meal, and all the other negatives that generally made us feel terrible). Then we began to associate immense amounts of satisfaction with the daily changes we had made (e.g., we enjoyed experiencing food as nourishment, rather than entertainment; we enjoyed our daily exercises, finding satisfaction in the small changes we were making in our bodies each day).

Taking Action

Once you decide to make a change in your life—once you have enough leverage—it's important to take immediate action toward making the change. This doesn't mean you must run ten miles to improve your health, or quit your job today to pursue your passions. Rather, you should take one step in the right direction. You must build some momentum first. Otherwise, you will experience large amounts of dissatisfaction and your change won't last.

These first few steps are crucial. Once you get enough momentum behind you the change becomes fun and exciting, and you want to continue to improve and grow. Thus, you want to find little ways to make improvements in each area of your life, be it exercising daily, strengthening your relationships via one meaningful conversation per day, spending one hour on whatever you're most passionate about, etc. These small changes add up quickly, and they compound on top of each other. And, pretty soon, you'll glance in the rearview and be stunned by how much progress you've made.

That's what happened to us. Over a few years, everything changed: we left our big corporate jobs, changed our diets, started exercising regularly, became healthy, strengthened our core relationships, made great new relationships, started cultivating our passions, and contributed to more people than we ever had before. We didn't know making this many changes was possible in such a short period of time, but when we look back at it, we're thankful we decided to take gradual, daily actions that changed everything for us in a relatively short period of time.

Raise Your Standards

What seemed impossible yesterday, will often seem easy tomorrow. So if you want to continue to grow, you must continue to raise your standards; otherwise, you'll plateau. Or worse, if you lower your standards, you'll atrophy.

While you're taking your daily incremental actions, it's important to raise the bar a little each day, especially when it's uncomfortable. Getting outside your comfort zone is an important part of growth. You needn't raise the bar too high, but just high enough to make your change a little more difficult each day. Over time, your gradually raised standards will add up to changes larger than you could have imagined.

For us, the most glaring example of raising our standards was with respect to our health. Once we made the decision to change our diet and exercise, and we started taking daily actions to improve both of these areas, we would also raise the bar just a little each day, especially with exercise. There was a point when neither of us exercised at all. In Joshua's case he couldn't do a single push-up or a single pull-up. At the beginning, he learned some techniques that allowed him to do modified versions of both exercises until one day he was able to do one of each. One push-up turned into two, which turned into ten, which eventually turned into over 100 in a row. The same was true for other exercises, as well. If he would have attempted 100 when he started, he would have failed. That failure would have presented with it a considerable amount of dissatisfaction, discouraging him from continuing his growth. He likely would have given up. Instead, he gradually raised the bar each day, building more and more on the achievements of days prior.

Consistent Actions

While you continue to raise your standards, it's important to focus on consistent action. Said another way, it's easier to raise the bar a little each day than raise it seven times as much each week or 30 times as much each month.

For example, it's important to strengthen your relationships each day. You will get more benefit from being nice to your lover today and tomorrow than you will from yelling at them today and buying them flowers tomorrow.

The same holds true for all areas of life: the key to real growth is consistency. Consistent, gradual action taken every day is the way we changed our lives. It feels like a slow climb at first, but once you build enough momentum, you won't want to stop growing. It's *growth* that makes you feel alive.

CHAPTER 6: CONTRIBUTION

The Importance of Contribution

Contribution is the most important of the Five Values. Don't believe us? Let us prove it.

Imagine winning the lottery, getting into the best shape of your life, finding your soulmate, establishing the most meaningful relationships possible, paying off your debts, moving into your dream home (on the beach, of course), finding the thing that makes you the most passionate, discovering your mission in life, and finding new ways to grow every day.

Now what? Bask in your wealth, fortune, and fame at the top of your mound of money, swimming through your cash and coins like Scrooge McDuck? Not hardly.

Growth Leads to Contribution

As you grow, something amazing tends to happen: you have more of yourself to give. It's an incredible cycle: the more you grow, the more you can help others grow; and the more you help others grow, the more you grow in return.

Beyond Yourself

Growth feels great, but contribution can feel even better. That's because you often do more for the people you love than you do for yourself.

The reason you're willing to do more for the people you love is that humans have an intrinsic need to contribute beyond themselves—contribution is a basic human instinct.

Ways to Contribute

A nice thing about contributing to other people is there are countless ways to do so. And there isn't a right or wrong way to contribute: all contribution is positive. Thus, it is important to learn how to best contribute to the people around you.

Later in this chapter, we'll discuss how the two of us contribute to local organizations, as well as online, but it's important to note that donating your time to these types of activities is not the only way to contribute. Instead, you can find tiny ways to contribute in many of your current activities.

In our past corporate lives, we both led large groups of people for a major corporation. In doing so, we both discovered the most rewarding part of our workday revolved around mentoring others: we felt the most fulfilled whenever we added value to other people's lives. Ergo, whether you're donating your time to a charity, or you're finding new ways to contribute to your primary relationships, you are doing one thing: adding value.

Adding Value

How does this task add value? This is a question we asked every day in our corporate jobs. More than anything else, this one question helped us succeed. We also asked our employees the same question: *How did you add value today?*

And now we still ask this question of ourselves each day.

At its core, this question helps you identify how you're contributing. If you don't have a good answer, then another question is appropriate: *How could I add value to this situation?* or *How could I better add value?* By asking these questions you begin to understand how to use your limited time to better contribute to the people around you.

For example, have you ever witnessed an inspiring short speech or monologue that made you want to take immediate action? Similarly, have you gone through a semester-long college or high school class that added the same amount of value to your life? If you're like most people, the answer is *yes* to both of these questions. But if you had the opportunity to add immense value to someone's life in one hour, doesn't that make more sense than stretching it out over weeks or months? Of course it does.

While this might seem like a drastic example, the point is to make the most of your interactions. If you're constantly asking yourself *How am I adding value?* you'll start getting some great answers. When you think in terms of adding value, you'll start to notice everything you do begins to add value in various ways. That's because over time you'll begin to weed out anything that doesn't add value to your own life or to other people's lives.

How We Contribute

We've found plenty of ways to contribute to people in our local community, as well as to people all over the world (via our website).

For example, locally we've donated our time to Habitat for Humanity, soup kitchens, and various charitable organizations. We've helped paint schools, raise money, clean up the streets, paint fire hydrants and parks, and helped the community in various other ways.

Furthermore, our website has garnered millions of readers from every country in the world, which has led to our collective contribution, including constructing an elementary school in Laos, installing clean-water wells in Malawi, funding a high school in Uganda for a year, building an orphanage in Honduras, and many similar projects throughout the world.

Thus, there are at least two ways you can contribute to others:

Local Organizations. You can contribute to local organizations who come together to contribute to your local community (e.g., Habitat for Humanity, Big Brothers Big Sisters, and various other nonprofit organizations, homeless shelters, soup kitchens, and the like). For a list of great places to start, visit volunteermatch.org or check out the classifieds in your local free community paper.

Start Your Own Thing. Many people discover so much satisfaction from contributing to others that it becomes important to them to create their own means by which to contribute. For us, this meant starting a website where we documented our journey and helped other people by sharing advice based on our personal experiences. For other people, this could mean any number of things: from starting a community garden to providing work-training to inner-city children. Typically, if you're going to start your own thing, you get there by contributing to local organizations first, determining how you can best add value in the process.

We subscribe to a combination of the two, because they fulfill us in different ways.

Donating our time to local nonprofit organizations allows us to connect with people face to face, as well as connect with the community as a whole.

Our website, on the other hand, allows us to contribute intellectually to a much larger group of people in ways not possible without the Internet.

Wherever you start, you'll likely need to start somewhere that's a little out of your comfort zone if you're not used to contributing in these ways. That's completely understandable. You'll want to explore different organizations—different locations with different people—until you find one that's right for you. It also helps to have some variety in the ways you help so your contribution efforts continue to feel fresh and exciting.

Big or Small Equals Satisfaction

The good news about contribution is no matter how you contribute, you get to feel an immense satisfaction from your contributions—a satisfaction like no other. We started contributing on a small scale, well before we had our website, by seeking out local charity events at which we could participate.

We would tag along with whatever group was donating their time and help however we could. After our first few events we discovered something unexpected: we felt really, really good about our contribution; contributing beyond ourselves gave us a deep sense of satisfaction we didn't experience from other aspects of our lives.

Writing Checks Is Not the Answer

We've heard some people say things like *I don't have time to donate my time to charity; I'll just write a check instead.* While donating money to charitable organizations is commendable (and we encourage you to do so if you can afford it), the satisfaction you get from such donations pales in comparison to actual engaged contribution. The face-to-face interactions, the physical exertion, and the mental activity of being completely immersed in contribution are far more rewarding than writing a check.

Two Types of Positive Experiences

There are two types of positive experiences in life:

Positive experiences you enjoy. For some people this category includes activities like playing a sport, teaching a child how to ride a bike, snowboarding, going to a friend's house to watch a football game, and the like. These are often the best and most effortless experiences in your life. They are easy to do because they are exciting, rewarding, fulfilling. Unfortunately, these types of experiences are rare compared to the second type of positive experiences.

Positive experiences you dislike. For some people this category includes most of the activities that are good for them, like eating vegetables, exercising daily, manual labor, conversing with loved ones each night, taking on new challenges.

Why People Don't Contribute

The reason people don't contribute as much as they should (or as much as they want) is because they often identify contributive experiences as positive experiences they dislike. And of course, humans have a natural tendency to avoid what they dislike. This must change if you are truly committed to experiencing lasting satisfaction and fulfillment.

The Key to Living Meaningfully

The second type of positive experiences—the positive experiences you dislike—are the key to living a meaningful life.

That is, finding ways to transform the positive experiences you dislike into positive experiences you enjoy is the ticket to changing your life long-term. This one strategy is the ticket to long-term happiness, fulfillment, and a life with meaning.

This strategy doesn't only enable you to change your relationship to contribution; it can be effective in every area of your life. We've waited until now to share this key element so that we can discuss ways it might be applied to all Five Values.

Health example. It's not easy to exercise each morning before an arduous workday. It's easier to get an extra 30 minutes of sleep. But you know without a doubt which experience is better for you: that morning exercise will start your day the right way, give you great momentum and energy for the day ahead, and will certainly serve you better than half an hour of sleep.

Relationship example. It's not easy to come home after a long day of work and engage in an hour of meaningful conversation with the people you love; it's far easier to get lost in the television's hypnotic luminescence. But, again, that evening conversation with your partner or close friends will strengthen your relationships and add far more value to your own life (not to mention their life) in ways TV never could.

Passion example. It's not easy to stay at home at night obsessively working on your passion while all your friends and coworkers are grabbing drinks at the local bar; it's easier to go out and have a few beers, eat a few nachos, and have ephemeral exchanges with these people.

Growth example. It's not easy to embrace new experiences like finding new ways to exercise or starting a new business or meeting new people; it's easier to keep doing what you're doing, to stay in your comfort zone, to avoid new creative endeavors because they might fail.

Contribution example. Similarly, with respect to contribution, it's not easy to get up on a Saturday morning and go work at a community event; it's easier to do a few chores around the house or turn on this season's sporting event or simply do nothing at all.

The point is that there will always be something there to tempt you from doing the things that make your life more meaningful. The good news is you can avoid those tempting activities by transforming the positive experiences you *dislike* into positive experiences you *enjoy*. In this way, all the positive experiences that relate to your life are made enjoyable. We have found ways to take the experiences that used to seem tedious to us and make them fun and exciting.

The Fun and Excitement of Contribution

No matter what activities the two of us do, we go out of our way to make sure we enjoy them. Whether engaging in activities related to our health, our relationships, our passions, our personal growth, or the ways in which we contribute to others, look for ways to make things playful, silly, exciting.

Contributing is a serious matter, but we don't take it too seriously. Rather, we're playful, we have fun with what we do, we enjoy the process of contributing. We do this by asking ourselves one question: *How could I make this experience enjoyable?* This sounds like an elementary question, but it is the foundation of turning the positive experiences we dislike into positive experiences we enjoy.

Try this: think of a way you could contribute beyond yourself (preferably in a way you've never contributed before). If you're at a loss, use the website we gave you earlier in this chapter: volunteermatch.org. Once you have your means of contribution, ask yourself *How could I make this experience enjoyable?* Write down the answers you come up with.

For example, a few weeks before writing this, the two of us worked with Habitat for Humanity on a chilly Saturday afternoon in late autumn, donating our time to help build a home for a family in Dayton, Ohio. As we stood outside, hanging siding on the house, cold rain began falling from the sky, soaking our clothes and our chipper demeanors. It wasn't pleasant. At least not at first. Ryan looked at Joshua and asked, "How could we make this enjoyable?" Although it was a basic question, the answer wasn't that easy—it's not easy to make cold rain and construction work enjoyable. So we started brainstorming as we continued hanging the siding: What if we got the kids from inside the home and asked them to help us? What if we raced to see who could hang the most siding the quickest? What if we sang aloud like a couple of idiots while we hung the siding? What if we did terrible impressions of Robert DeNiro and Christopher Walken working construction? What if we did jumping jacks in the rain every five minutes to take a break from the construction work? What if we went inside until the rain let up, made hot chocolate for everyone, and told stories to the family? Then we could get them to help us finish the siding when the rain stopped. What if, what if, what if?

Within a few minutes we had over a dozen answers, most of which were quite silly. But we picked a few and gave them a shot, increasing the level of enjoyment for an otherwise mundane task. We joked, we laughed, and we had a good time. We turned a dull activity into something we enjoyed—a great day of contribution, something we won't forget for a long time.

Giving Is Living

Unless you contribute beyond yourself, your life will feel perpetually self-serving. It's okay to operate in your own self-interest, but doing so exclusively creates an empty existence. A life without contribution is a life without meaning. The truth is that giving is living. We feel truly alive only when we are growing and contributing. That's what a real life is all about. That's what it means to live a meaningful life—a life filled with great health, great relationships, and ultimate passion.

CHAPTER 7: CONFLUENCE

The Most Important Value?

Throughout the five previous chapters, we explored the Five Values of living a meaningful life. You probably noticed we started each chapter by presenting you with reasons why that particular value was the most important of the five. Truth be told, all five are tremendously important. But which area is the most important?

This is a question we have asked ourselves plenty of times, and we tend to reach a different conclusion each time we ask. The honest answer is all Five Values are equally important. The more precise answer is the importance of each value changes over time for each of us. Thus, we all experiences stages—be it brief or lengthy, a day or a month—in which the importance of a particular value takes priority over another.

A Person's Top Two Values

We've noticed over time there are often two values that rise to the top of a person's priority list. In other words, of the Five

Values, you'll tend to make two of them a priority. That is to say that even though every person will shift all Five Values—invariably making any of the five a top priority at any particular time—they will have two values that rise to the top considerably more often than the other three. Again, this can vary drastically depending on the person and their desires and beliefs.

Joshua's Top Two Values

For Joshua, the two areas of his life that tend to receive the most focus are health and passion. He fulfills his passion by writing every morning as soon as he gets out of bed (read his essay "Why I Wake at 3:30 AM" at minimalists.com/morning), and he focuses on his health daily by eating healthy foods and exercising. These things come almost naturally for him, but they didn't always. Once he developed habits he enjoyed, though, focusing on these two areas of his life became the easiest.

That isn't to say that the other three areas—relationships, growth, contribution—are ignored. They're not. But it's important to know which two areas are your current default values, because then you can focus on the other three that come less naturally. Joshua knows he must make a concerted effort to focus on his relationships, his personal growth, and contributing to others each day. By focusing on the values that come less naturally, he is able to better balance his life.

Ryan's Top Two Values

For Ryan, relationships and growth reign supreme. As an extreme extrovert, Ryan loves being around people, and fostering relationships comes naturally to him. Similarly, Ryan's competitive nature forces him to compete with himself, promoting rapid personal growth. This means Ryan must make a daily effort to focus on his bottom three values: health, passion, and contribution.

Bottom Three Values

It's important to note that just because a person has two values on which they focus most, that doesn't make the bottom three less important. In fact, the opposite can be true. If someone focuses too much on one or two particular areas of their life, then the remaining areas may lack the attention they need, resulting in an unbalanced and unsatisfied life.

For example, if a man focuses all his energy on his health and pursuing his passions, and places too little emphasis on his relationships, then there's a good chance he will feel lonely and depressed. If he avoids growing, then he will feel stuck and complacent—a spinning wheel. If he sidesteps contributing, then he will always feel a certain amount of discontent, for we only experience real fulfillment when we contribute beyond ourselves.

Balancing All Five Values

Understanding your top two values is important, but balance among all five is paramount. The only way to experience long-term contentment is to focus on all Five Values.

To do so, we recommend incorporating each of the Five Values into your *daily* life, because making all five areas the core of your everyday life is the best way to ensure you are living a meaningful life.

The best way to do this is to simply ask yourself a question:

How did I incorporate all Five Values into my life today? That is: *How did I focus on health, relationships, passion, growth, and contribution?*

Once we are aware of how we incorporate these five areas into our daily lives, we become acutely aware of how we are spending our time.

With every action we take, the two of us tend to ask ourselves the following question: *Which area of my life does this action improve?* If it doesn't improve any of the five areas, then we need to ask another question: *How could this task improve one of the five important areas of my life?* If whatever you're doing doesn't improve at least one of the five areas—directly or indirectly—then it's important to find a way to drastically reduce or eliminate that action from your daily life.

Most people's days are filled with tedious, banal tasks that take up much of their time but don't add value to their lives. We could provide a million examples of daily tasks that do not lend themselves to intentional living, but here are a few obvious examples:

Smoking. Obviously, smoking is bad for your health (so not only does it not improve that area of your life, it actually has a negative effect). Furthermore, smoking doesn't add value to your personal relationships; it doesn't help you pursue your passions; it certainly doesn't help you grow; nor does it help you contribute to other people.

Overeating. Similar to smoking, eating too much is harmful to your health, and it doesn't contribute to any of the other areas of your life.

Gossip. Talking negatively about others can damage your relationships. Plus, it obviously doesn't fuel any of the other four values.

There are myriad examples of everyday activities people do that do not positively contribute to their lives.

Take ten minutes and write down all the things you've done in the last week that do not contribute to the five important areas of your life. Now write down why they don't contribute to any of those five areas. How can you reduce or eliminate these activities from your life?

The Role of Minimalism

So we finally get back to minimalism. We knew it had to be somewhere in this book other than in the opening chapters, right? You might be thinking, how does minimalism come to play in all this?

We'd like to posit to you that minimalism plays a substantial role in living a meaningful life. Recall our definition from the first chapter: *Minimalism is a tool to eliminate life's excess and focus on the essentials.* Therefore, this book is about minimalism, because this book is about focusing on the five essential areas of life. By embracing minimalism in other aspects of life (your possessions, your work, etc.), you can focus on the most important things in life (the Five Values).

Thus, living a meaningful life and minimalism go hand in hand. Minimalism acts as a tool, helping you focus on what's important much more easily; it clears away the clutter so you can focus on living more deliberately.

What excess items, tasks, and relationships can you remove

from your life so you can focus more of your time and energy on all Five Values?

(For practical decluttering tips, visit our "Start Here" page at minimalists.com/start to start your own journey.)

A More Meaningful Life

It's also important to ask another question about your daily tasks: *How could this task positively affect one or more of the five important areas of my life?* By asking better questions like this, we get better answers.

Not everything you do is as black and white as smoking or gossip; some daily tasks can be questionable. For example, watching television. There's nothing wrong with watching TV per se, but if it consumes a large amount of your time, then it can be detrimental to living a meaningful life. So, instead, ask yourself, *How could watching television better influence one or more areas of my life?* Perhaps you could schedule your viewing time with a friend, watching your favorite show together, and then afterward the two of you could discuss what happened. The two of us do this with our favorite TV shows. This way we're not stuck in the state of perpetual channel surfing that can consume large amounts of time without adding any value to your life. Or perhaps you can watch TV while you spend an hour on an elliptical machine, improving your physical health.

With many questionable items, there is often more than one way to make it positively affect at least one of the Five Values. If you can't think of a way to turn one of your questionable items into something that impacts one of the Five Values, then you should probably remove (or drastically reduce) that item from your life. It's important to be honest with yourself when considering what things to remove from your life; doing so will provide you with the best possible outcome. Removing certain things from your life might be difficult at first, but the rewards you enjoy are worth the momentary sacrifice.

Other examples of questionable items include things like spending time on the Internet, social media, shopping, daily drive-time to and from work, sleeping in too late, and staying awake too late at night.

What other questionable items take away your time? Make a list. How can you make these tasks positively impact one or more areas of your life?

Maximizing Results

Some of the things we do positively influence more than one of the Five Values. Often, these are some of the best activities to help you live more meaningfully.

For example, we enjoy exercising together, which positively affects our health and our relationship. We enjoy working on our website together, which positively affects our relationship, helps us grow, allows us to contribute to other people, and permits us to actively engage in our passions. In these two examples alone, we cover all Five Values of living a meaningful life. That's because some activities allow us to maximize our results.

What activities do you do that influence more than one of the Five Values? What can you do to make your current activities influence more of the Five Values at once?

How Do You Know?

How do you know if you're living a meaningful life?

This is an important question. Unfortunately, there is no

binary answer. There is no checklist or set of absolute maxims by which you must gauge your life to answer this question—just like there is no way to definitively answer many questions in life. Am I healthy? Am I happy? Am I content? Am I successful? Am I smart? Am I passionate? Am I growing? Am I contributing beyond myself? Am I a good person?

You might be thinking, *Great, so I'm almost at the end of the book, and you're not going to tell me if I'm living a meaningful life?*

No, we're not going to tell you. Actually, we *can't* tell you. Only you know for sure.

Just as with the aforementioned questions, there are different sets of criteria and internal rules each of us place on those questions. We might think you're smart or good or happy, but what we think doesn't matter. Only you know for sure.

The way we measure our success in each of the Five Values is through a simple equation, an equation we call the Simple Success Formula:

Success = Happiness + Constant Improvement

This equation applies to any of the Five Values. Ultimately, you are successful in any of these five areas of life if you are happy with where you currently are and if you are constantly improving that area of your life.

For example, you may not be in the best shape, but if you are happy with the progress you've made, and you're happy with your daily improvements, then you are successful in that area of your life. Conversely, if you are in great shape, but you are not improving your health in tiny ways each day, then you won't feel successful in the long run. Or, if you're not happy with your physical shape, but you are constantly improving, then you aren't yet successful in that area of your life, but you are likely on the road to success if you are making small daily improvements to your overall health.

Similarly, if you're not happy with your relationships and you are not making any improvements in that area, you are unsuccessful. For the two of us, this was the case for all Five Values just a few years ago. If you go back and read the first chapter, you'll notice that neither of us were happy with our lives —neither of us were happy with our health, our relationships, our passions, our personal growth, or how we contributed to others. What's worse, we also weren't improving these areas of our lives. In fact, if anything, these areas were further deteriorating as we journeyed down the paths we were traveling, building our discontent over time.

This is when we decided to take back control of our lives. We used the principles of minimalism to eliminate the excess stuff in our lives so we could focus on the Five Values every day. Over the course of two years, everything changed for us. We got rid of the superfluous in favor of the essential—in favor of a more meaningful life.

None of this was easy. It takes daily focus and a commitment to constant improvement. And to continue living a meaningful life, we must continue to commit to constantly improving each area of our lives. We must do so every day. Small daily improvements make all the difference.

What we discovered over the past several years is that we can be happy, we can improve our lives every day, and, ultimately, we can live meaningful lives—and so can you.

ABOUT THE MINIMALISTS

JOSHUA FIELDS MILLBURN & RYAN NICODEMUS are bestselling authors and international speakers who share their message about living a meaningful life with less stuff. Their story has been featured on the *Today* show and in *Time*, *People*, *Forbes*, *New York Times*, *Wall Street Journal*, *USA Today*, *Boston Globe*, *San Francisco Chronicle*, *Chicago Tribune*, *Seattle Times*, *Toronto Star*, *Globe & Mail*, *Vancouver Sun*, *Village Voice*, *LA Weekly*, and many other outlets. Visit the authors online at *TheMinimalists.com*.